THE SMALL COLLEGE MEETS THE CHALLENGE

The Story of CASC

ALFRED T. HILL

Executive Secretary
The Council for the Advancement of Small Colleges, Inc.
Washington, D.C.

McGRAW-HILL BOOK COMPANY, INC.

New York   Toronto   London

1959

THE SMALL COLLEGE MEETS THE CHALLENGE

FOREWORD

It was my privilege to be one of the "attending physicians" at the birth of a new educational organization—CASC. I conferred with the founders when they held their organizational meeting in Chicago in April, 1956, and also served as a consultant at the first workshop of CASC held on the campus of Nasson College in Springvale, Maine, later that year.

Since that time, as a member of CASC's board of advisors, I have watched with increasing interest and enthusiasm the development of this sturdy young enterprise. The purpose of this organization is worthy, and its achievements to date have been outstanding.

The account which Dr. Hill gives in the following pages is a readable record of what a group of small colleges can do to help themselves and of what they can do to gain the support and endorsement of strong friends.

The potential represented by the majority of the members of this unique association is of importance to American higher education now and in the years ahead. One of the impressive facts brought out by this book is that in the college field, just as in industry and elsewhere, problems can best be solved by the exercise of originality and initiative.

This is the story of grass-roots institutions, close to their communities, staffed by dedicated teachers, and attended by serious-minded young men and women. This book constitutes a significant contribution to the current literature on higher education.

Theodore A. Distler
ASSOCIATION OF AMERICAN COLLEGES
EXECUTIVE DIRECTOR

PREFACE

Although the title of this book is *The Small College Meets the Challenge,* its unique feature is implied by its subtitle, *The Story of CASC.* In the following pages, the sixty-five members of the Council for the Advancement of Small Colleges are regarded from two viewpoints: first, as individuals grouped together in a unique organization for a special purpose and, second, as a small but important segment of the whole circle of higher education in America.

One important fact about this group of colleges is that they are typical of a much larger number of rather similar small institutions which are not organized because they have no special cause to fight for. Many of the facts, figures, observations, and conclusions regarding the CASC colleges might very well, with minor modifications, apply to scores of other colleges. In effect, CASC has been running a sort of experimental "pilot project," with implications far beyond the limits of its own membership.

Perhaps the most important contribution that this observer has gained from a study of these colleges is the significance of their group impact upon the major educational problems of our day. No single small institution with fewer than five hundred students and a span of existence of something like fifty years is likely to stir the depths of the ocean of higher education. However, a group of such colleges scattered through thirty-one states and serving a great variety of interests promotes what President Eisenhower has called the American tradition of diversity and independence. These colleges should be strengthened, encouraged, recognized, and appreciated both for what they are doing now and for the potentiality they represent in the future.

To become very personal for a moment, I wish to acknowledge with gratitude the privilege which has been mine in working with the colleges of CASC. The dedicated efforts and wise leadership of its president, K. Duane Hurley, the conscientiousness of the board of directors, and the energetic responsiveness of all the members have contributed to making my association with CASC an exceptionally fine professional experience. I also wish to acknowledge the valuable advice and influence of the board of advisors, whose names are listed opposite the title page. The hard work, wise counsel, and public sponsorship of these men have been of the greatest importance in helping this unusual group of colleges to increase the effectiveness of their service to American youth. Finally, I wish to express my heartfelt thanks to Paul L. Zens, staff associate, and Dora M. Staples, administrative assistant, in the Washington office. Without their painstaking efforts and unusual patience with the author, these pages might never have seen the light of day.

Alfred T. Hill

CONTENTS

Chapter 1

THE FORGOTTEN COLLEGES

The Noise You Hear Is Progress. . . . Let's start a fund for the forgotten colleges. . . . We must break the vicious circle. . . . Operation Bootstrap. . . . The in-group of the have-nots. . . . How to raise a million dollars. . . . Small colleges an untapped resource. . . . Advancing quality education. . . .

These are only a few of the labels, slogans, and catch phrases which filled the air and made the headlines in connection with the birth of a new educational association—the Council for the Advancement of Small Colleges—CASC.

Why should such an organization come into existence? Of what importance is it to present or future college students? Does it solve any problems for weary parents scanning the headlines and wondering whether any college will be ready for Willie and Mary by the time they are ready for college? Does it have the answer for the corporation executive who scratches his head in bewilderment and says, "I know nothing about the technical side of education and yet I'm besieged constantly with requests for money from national educational groups, regional groups, state groups, and individual institutions—what to do?" Does this organization meet any special challenge?

These are realistic questions. They are important. They deserve honest answers. This book answers them.

This is a book by the executive secretary of the Council for the Advancement of Small Colleges. It tells about the role of a particular group of small but important colleges on the vast stage of American higher education in the mid-twentieth century. It is written as a message to the public, as an observation of a social phenomenon, as an explanation of a situation, as a

1

description of a group of colleges, and as an analytical estimate of their present contribution and future potentiality in the face of a critical national need.

The term "small college" is used for all colleges with enrollments of fewer than a thousand students. However, the point should be established at the beginning of this discussion that the colleges here referred to are the sixty-five members of CASC. They are used as a representative sample of a much larger group of institutions of roughly similar size. The unique fact about these sixty-five colleges is that they are organized for the specific purpose of *advancing* small colleges.

WHAT CHALLENGE?

These colleges have discovered that in attempting to solve their own particular problems they are contributing to the solution of national problems far beyond the limits of their own organized membership. They are focusing attention upon the unique potential of all small colleges. In short, this book tells how the small college meets its challenges.

First there is the challenge of quantity. Between 1955 and 1970 enrollments are expected to double, from 3 to 6 million students. This fact alone leads to other problems—not enough dormitories, classrooms, libraries, laboratories, and other physical facilities and not enough teachers.

Second there is the challenge of quality. The first place to get good quality is in the education, experience, personality, and dedication of the college faculties. The second place is in the adequate college preparation of entering students. The third place is in the content, methods, and academic standards of the curriculum.

All the statements above lead to the third main challenge— money, not "finances," but good old-fashioned cash. How much is education going to cost? Who is going to pay the bill?

A fourth challenge is implied by the current confusion about how to judge a good college. This breaks down into such considerations as financial stability, academic standards, regional accreditation, cost to students, community service, educational experimentation, etc., *ad infinitum.*

And finally there is the challenge of diversity and independence in American higher education. Are we going to follow the trend of bigness, bureaucracy, and Federal support plus Federal control—all of which imply conformity, inefficiency, and extravagance? Or are we going to hold out for the little man, the individual, the nonconformist? Are we going to emphasize the opportunities for Americans to solve their own problems by using their wits, their imagination, their courage in the development of the available resources?

These are only a few of the elements in the challenge which the small colleges are meeting.

THE SMALL COLLEGE—AN UNTAPPED RESOURCE

It was only natural under these circumstances for thoughtful persons to raise further questions as to how the challenge of expansion was to be met. Should it be through enlarging existing institutions, starting new ones, merging groups of small ones, shifting various functions? This was one obvious question: are there any existing colleges which represent an undeveloped resource which could be expanded at relatively low cost?

The Council for the Advancement of Small Colleges answers this last question with a resounding *yes.* The council came into existence in April, 1956, in response to a widespread and urgent demand. This demand was expressed by a group of the so-called forgotten colleges; i.e., they were not literally forgotten, but they were excluded from the financial benefits of the 260-million-dollar grant made by the Ford Foundation in December, 1955, to 630 colleges for the improvement of faculty salaries. Why were these colleges excluded? Because for various reasons they had not achieved membership in one of the six regional accrediting associations of the country.

And why had they not achieved such membership?

Dr. Benjamin Fine, former education editor of *The New York Times,* writing on June 17, 1956, had this to say on college accreditation:

> The major regional accrediting bodies are the Middle States Association of Colleges and Secondary Schools, the North Central Association of Colleges and Secondary Schools, the New England Association of Colleges and Secondary Schools, the Northwest Association of Secondary and Higher Schools, the Southern Association of Colleges and Secondary Schools, and the Western College Association.
>
> Various criteria are used by these groups. Among them are a strong curriculum, sound teaching methods, library facilities, and financial solvency. Money is extremely important; colleges with excellent faculties have been denied accreditation solely because they lacked sufficient endowment or could not show over-all solvency.
>
> Accreditation is important. Even though a college that does not have the seal of approval of its regional accrediting agency may be doing a good teaching job, it is seriously handicapped. For one thing, graduate schools frequently deny admittance to students who come from an unaccredited college. So students may not go to a nonaccredited institution except as a last resort.

In a bulletin of March, 1957, *The Small Non-Accredited College: Its Place in American Higher Education,* the Council for Financial Aid to Education took this position:

> For the most part the colleges lacking regional accreditation need—and would benefit from—larger enrollments, greater endowments, more adequate plant facilities, more books in their libraries, and more scholars on their faculties. Some were established a century ago. Others are only a few years old. . . .
>
> Many others are constantly gaining and with moderate help, educational and financial, may be expected to achieve accreditation. Many have good leadership, competent administration, acceptable academic programs, dedicated teachers, and on the whole students of at least average ability. With relatively inexpensive improvements many of these colleges evidently can meet

the requirements of accreditation and thus at small additional cost carry a much heavier share of the present and future enrollment load.

It has been estimated that these small colleges, within their existing capacities, can provide educational opportunity to tens of thousands of additional students at an additional cost of a small fraction of the cost of providing equivalent opportunity through installation of completely new institutions.

SIMILARITIES OR DIFFERENCES?

These statements may seem to indicate a wide disparity between the "haves" and the "have-nots." On the other hand, a close examination would reveal stronger similarities than differences. As one college president expressed it, "The problems of the non-regionally accredited colleges are the same as those of all other colleges only multiplied by the factor X." This is true. For example, both groups are under pressure to accept more students; both are making every effort to improve faculty salaries; both are engaged in extensive building programs; both need to improve their financial stability in a variety of ways; both are interested in better business management of their non-academic affairs; and both are concerned about advancing quality education.

Comparisons made by William K. Selden, executive secretary of the National Commission on Accrediting, between a group of small regionally accredited colleges and a group of non-regionally accredited colleges tend to underscore their similarities.[1] Their average enrollments are approximately the same —fewer than four hundred students. The majority are church-related. Predominantly they are non-tax-supported. Their average age is seventy-five years. They are widely distributed geographically. Their most pressing problems are financial.

[1] William K. Selden, "Whither the Small College?" Association of American Colleges *Bulletin,* vol. 52, no. 2, pp. 267–270, May, 1956.

THE VICIOUS CIRCLE

It is no wonder in the light of this situation that K. Duane Hurley, president of Salem College, Salem, West Virginia, was quoted in an article in *Time* (March 5, 1956) as saying that these colleges were caught in a vicious circle—"you need accreditation to get money, and money to get accreditation."

And so it came about that a group of these institutions met in Chicago and founded the Council for the Advancement of Small Colleges, Inc., with Dr. Hurley as its first president. They did this in order to achieve certain goals collectively and by cooperation which were beyond their means individually. One of these goals was regional accreditation. Another was increased financial support. A third was the improvement of their academic programs. A fourth was an increase in their *visibility* to the public. And still another which soon became apparent was to conduct educational experiments appropriate to their own needs. In promoting these objectives the council has helped to meet the challenge of the national crisis in higher education.

AS OTHERS SEE US

We have been told that it is wise to try to see ourselves as others see us. Therefore, it seems appropriate to let James Sunshine of the Providence *Journal-Bulletin* describe CASC as he saw it in the spring of 1957 when it was one year old:[2]

Like the man who sought treasure abroad only to find it at home, the nation is beginning to discover "space" in colleges it scarcely knew existed a year or two ago.

The discovery is being made chiefly at the insistence of the discovered institutions, some fifty-three private four-year liberal arts colleges which, to call attention to themselves, have banded together as the Council for the Advancement of Small Colleges.

These institutions intend to raise money, improve their stand-

[2] James K. Sunshine, Providence, R.I., *Journal-Bulletin*, Apr. 18–19, 1957.

ards, enlarge their facilities, and gain accreditation. When this is done, they will be able to offer themselves as respectable collegiate havens to the thousands of qualified youths who will be knocking, without much hope, on the doors of better-known institutions within a few years. . . .

The story of the council is fascinating largely because it fits so well into the standard, but now somewhat debilitated, American tradition of starting with virtually nothing and building from the ground up.

Most of these institutions are poor and struggling. They literally have no bank accounts worth the name. Their buildings are sometimes made-over houses and sometimes barns. Their students are sometimes very good and sometimes not so good. Their faculties are inclined to be short on Ph.D.s but long on idealism. Often their curricula are good but frankly experimental; sometimes they are unquestionably inadequate. Often, the ordinary accessories of collegiate life—fraternities, football teams, yearbooks, and class life—are missing.

But, the argument runs, they are institutions with going programs, administrations, and heating plants. They can be expanded to accommodate twice and three times their present enrollments. Their standards can be raised. Moreover, since they are small and unfettered by tradition, they are in an excellent position to take on the job of educating students who might not fit into larger and more formal institutions, and also to bring back into American higher education the willingness for frank experimentation that once characterized it and gave it vitality.

A Modest Start

Harvard, Yale, and Brown were once like this, though their alumni might acknowledge the fact today only with some reluctance. But these institutions were built several centuries ago when pioneering was an obvious course of action in a young country. In the day of giant, billion-dollar corporations, the barehanded establishment of an institution of learning is less common. . . .

. . . .

Two hundred years ago, when an American living on the frontier wanted to raise a new barn, he called in the neighbors.

All shared in the work, and in the space of a single day the job was done. . . .

Stationed on the frontier of education, where living is thin and bank accounts are low, these colleges are seeking to do as a group what no one of them could do on its own.

In the year since the Council for the Advancement of Small Colleges was formed, its voice has begun to be heard. The steps of its officials have sounded in the halls of some of the large corporations, in some cases with noteworthy success.

Business firms that would have coldly turned down a request for funds from an unknown college are responding to the call of an ambitious and energetic organization of unknowns. Foundations are also coming through, in sharp contrast to the time two years ago when the Ford Foundation contributed 260 million dollars to virtually every accredited private college in the United States, leaving unaccredited institutions precisely where they were—in staggering difficulty. . . .

.   .   .   .

Educators and college administrators are greatly concerned with what they describe as "the coming tidal wave of students." This, it is estimated, will within a decade or so deposit 6 million college students on the doorsteps of the nation's institutions of higher education. There are only 3 million college students today, and most institutions are at peak enrollment. Where the overflow will go is anybody's guess.

Dr. Alfred T. Hill, executive secretary of the Council for the Advancement of Small Colleges, has one partial answer:

"How would the picture look," he suggested recently, "if we were to discover some available resources which had not been developed to their maximum potentialities? Suppose there were fifty small colleges distributed throughout the country with a possibility of doubling or even tripling their enrollments in the next five years.

"Suppose that they were alert to the situation and had the initiative to organize a self-help society. Suppose they dedicated themselves to strengthening their faculties, improving the teaching methods in their classrooms, conducting experiments leading to more interesting, vital, and realistic curricula.

"Imagine what it would mean if they could provide not only

more but better classrooms, libraries, laboratories, dormitories, and other facilities than they now have. Consider for a moment the fact that it would cost about ten times as much to replace these colleges if they were allowed to die as it would to double their effectiveness by capitalizing on their existing resources in plant, personnel, leadership, and experience."

Organized Last Year

The council was organized a year ago this month as a voluntary association of four-year private liberal arts colleges committed to an active development program leading to accreditation in the six great regional associations.

Without regional accreditation, they have been unable to obtain money; without money they have been unable to obtain accreditation. . . .

. . . .

It would be a mistake to assume that, even with generous support and better standards, member colleges of the council will be transmuted into duplicates of Harvard and Yale. It cannot be assumed that all would want this. Nor are they all interested in growing to vast size. Many of them, in fact, feel that the small college has and will continue to have advantages unmatched by the great traditional universities.

For one thing, small size has given them the freedom to achieve diversity. One of them, for example, offers a bachelor's degree in three years; another has an undergraduate major in forestry; a third offers advanced standing to superior students and has no class attendance regulations. One has an astronomical observatory and is one of the satellite "watch stations." Another is experimenting with the philosophy of John Dewey at the college level. Some have religious connections they feel are important and worth retaining. . . .

. . . .

In a summary of the council's first year, Dr. K. Duane Hurley, president of Salem College, Salem, West Virginia, whose outraged reaction to the "forgetfulness" of the Ford Foundation began the whole thing, happily ate his own words:

"A year ago," he declared, "I noted that these forgotten colleges were trapped in a vicious circle. Without regional accreditation they could not get money; without money they could not get regional accreditation. Now it looks as though the circle were starting to crack."

"THE NOISE YOU HEAR IS PROGRESS"

These immortal words were printed on a sign at the Palmer House in Chicago when CASC held its initial organization meeting in April, 1956. The management of the hotel was apologizing to its guests for the noisy repairs being conducted at the time. CASC hereby apologizes to the Palmer House for stealing the phrase which has become its slogan.

The council started at absolute zero with a meeting of some seventy-five college presidents who had never heard of each other before. Their progress from April, 1956, to April, 1959, may be briefly summarized as follows:

Organization. The council has adopted a constitution, elected officers and directors, become incorporated, established its tax exemption, and it has staffed, equipped, and operated an executive office in Washington.

Membership. The average membership has consisted of sixty-five colleges in thirty-one states.

Research. The council has compiled a comprehensive file of replies to questionnaires from its members covering such items as enrollment, finances, alumni support, campus news, student test scores, progress toward accreditation, etc. In addition, it has on file catalogues from all members, progress reports, and numerous self-surveys.

Coordination. The council has conducted three national meetings, four workshops, nine regional meetings, and quarterly directors' meetings. In addition, it has been represented at (and in many cases participated in) most of the regional and national meetings held by such groups as the Association of American Colleges, the American Council on Education, the American Alumni Council, the American College Public Relations Association, the Council for Financial Aid to Education, the Association for Higher Education (NEA), and various conferences called by the U.S. Office of Education (HEW).

Public Relations. Articles about the council and its members have appeared in over a dozen professional journals, in commercial magazines, such as *Time, Newsweek, Better Homes and Gardens, Glamour,* and *Changing Times,* in all the major metropolitan newspapers, and in many small newspapers. Council programs have been carried on radio and television in all parts of the country. The council has published a monthly newsletter and two directories (one for prospective students and one for prospective donors).

Regional Accreditation. Seven of the charter members have been accepted into full membership in their regional associations, and an eighth (a Negro college) received approval before the end of 1958. These colleges are Hillyer College, the New England Association of Colleges and Secondary Schools—December, 1956; Westmont College, Western College Association—March, 1958; College of St. Mary, Dana College, Edgewood College of the Sacred Heart, Morris Harvey, and Sioux Falls College, all admitted to the North Central Association of Colleges and Secondary Schools—March, 1958; Oakwood College, Southern Association of Colleges and Secondary Schools—December, 1958.

Advancing Quality Education. Progress has been made in this area through workshops concerned with a reexamination of fundamental purposes, curriculum experimentation, and business management. The colleges have used the area tests of the Graduate Record Examination to test sophomores and seniors and the College Qualification Tests to classify entering freshmen. Twenty-five members have availed themselves of special consultant services for improvement of curriculum and for accreditation. The council has now been organized under three commissions concerned with fund raising, academic improvement, and experimentation.

Fund Raising. The council has received financial support from the following:

The Alcoa Foundation	$1,000
Anonymous individual donor	1,000
The Concora Foundation	1,000
Esso Education Foundation	25,000
Ford Motor Company Fund	5,000
The Fund for the Advancement of Education	82,000
General Electric Company	27,500
Harbison-Walker Charitable Fund, Inc.	100
Harris Upham and Company	100
International Business Machines Corporation	500
The International Nickel Company, Inc.	5,000
The Koppers Foundation	500
National Biscuit Company Foundation	2,000
Olin Mathieson Chemical Corporation	5,000
Philip Morris Incorporated	1,000
Pitney-Bowes, Inc.	5,000
Remington-Rand (equipment) .	1,000
The Sears-Roebuck Foundation	15,000
Shell Companies Foundation	8,000
Simplex Wire & Cable Co.	500
Socony-Mobil Oil Company, Inc.	2,500
Thomson and McKinnon	100
Time, Incorporated	10,000
The Union Carbide and Carbon Educational Fund	27,500
United States Steel Foundation, Inc.	22,500
Woods Charitable Fund, Inc.	1,000
Total	$249,800

Future Plans. The board has approved a second term of three years for the council with the same general purposes and methods but a heavier concentration upon fund raising.

The individual members of the council have felt that their organization has been helpful in assisting them to achieve regional accreditation, raise money, increase enrollments, become better known, and to improve their academic programs.

From the national point of view, however, perhaps the greatest contribution CASC has made to date is to call the attention of the public in general and a number of key foundations, corporations, and individuals to the potentialities of this undeveloped resource. This has made good sense to the average business executive because it resembled a familiar practice, the staffing and general development of a small plant or branch of an organization in order to supply an increased demand. One way in which this situation was brought to the attention of business and industry was through the private printing and wide distribution of a handbook, *Small Colleges: An Untapped Resource.* This 24-page booklet contained information on the nature and purposes of the group as a whole, tables of statistical information, and a brief descriptive paragraph about each member college.

Since the sources of financial support are by no means the only ones in the country who need more information about these colleges, CASC has published *A Directory of Small Colleges* for the benefit of parents, school principals, guidance counselors, and prospective college students. This directory has received wide distribution under separate cover and constitutes Appendix B to this book. The book itself reports the present practices and indicates the future potentialities of these colleges and puts them in proper perspective relative to the broad general field of higher education.

IN GOOD COMPANY

CASC began in good company by holding its first meeting in Chicago along with the North Central Association of Colleges and Secondary Schools. Among those who addressed the CASC presidents were Robert E. Wilson, president of Standard Oil Company (Indiana); Frank H. Sparks, then chairman of the board and former president of Wabash College; Theodore A. Distler, executive director of the Association of American Colleges; Lewis B. Mayhew, dean of Michigan State University; William K. Selden, executive secretary of the National Commission on Accrediting, and representatives from several other organizations, including the Council for Financial Aid to Education.

This precedent of keeping good company has been followed out consistently. At the first workshop of CASC held on the campus of Nasson College in Springvale, Maine, the small colleges received advice and inspiration from fifteen speakers, all distinguished in their various fields of college finances, public relations, management, housing, and educational experimentation.

CASC has continued the practice of keeping good company through all its workshops, regional meetings, national meetings, and particularly through the establishment of its board of advisors.

Friendly cooperation has been received from all six regional associations, as well as from the Association of American Colleges, the American Council on Education, the Association of Higher Education (NEA), the American Alumni Council, the American College Public Relations Association, the Council for Financial Aid to Education, and the U.S. Office of Education (HEW). Boasting? Well, yes, these are friends worth boasting about.

CASC is particularly proud of the three following endorsements:

> The committee recommends that encouragement and support be given to worthy small colleges which are endeavoring to augment their resources sufficiently to enable them to achieve accreditation, which will further enable them to attract and meet the needs of additional students with little expansion of their present, underutilized facilities and faculties.
> The President's Committee on Education beyond the High School.

> The Waldorf Astoria Towers
> New York, New York
> May 2, 1957

Dear Dr. Hurley:

I have long been convinced that the failure of our great foundations to develop and support adequately the some fifty small non-accredited colleges is the greatest gap in their otherwise great contribution to American education.

These are colleges close to the people. They have served our people for long years through dedicated and self-denying teachers. Their intimate relations with the students enable them to do a better job in character building than our great institutions with their high attendance.

Their students come from those unable to meet the costs of the larger institutions. They represent an already invested capital of 65 million dollars, and they are providing for about 25,000 students.

We are short of higher educational facilities in every state for enlargement of mind and professional training, and students are being turned away every autumn.

To put these small colleges on their feet would probably cost less than 75 million dollars, which is probably not 10 per cent of the annual gifts to our larger institutions.

You have my best wishes for success in the council's efforts.

Yours faithfully,
Herbert Hoover

Council for the Advancement of Small Colleges
726 Jackson Place, N.W.
Washington 6, D.C.

Dear Dr. Hurley:

Please give my greetings to the directors of the Council for the Advancement of Small Colleges gathered in their second annual meeting.

Diversity and independence are distinguishing characteristics of American society and they are reflected in our traditions of higher education. In this setting our small colleges play an important role in meeting the expanding needs of students across the land.

Congratulations to the distinguished members of your newly formed board of advisers, and best wishes for the continued success of your efforts.

Dwight D. Eisenhower
April 3, 1958

SUMMARY

This chapter has presented a bird's-eye view of CASC—its history, purposes, and friends.

The potentialities of the colleges individually and the impact of the group as a whole will be discussed in the following chapters. It should be clear from the foregoing pages that CASC was organized in response to a genuine need. It is indeed dedicated to the purpose of helping the small college meet the challenge. As a result of its first three years of activity, CASC has increased the *visibility* of its members to such an extent that they can no longer be called the *forgotten colleges*.

Chapter 2

POTENTIALITY OF THE SMALL COLLEGE

DIVERSITY AND INDEPENDENCE

The membership of CASC, if considered in terms of its range and scope, is truly a cross section of private higher education in America. The President's Committee on Education beyond the High School in its *First Interim Report* identified four basic elements in American education under these headings: *quantity, quality, variety,* and *accessibility.* CASC colleges exhibit these characteristics in the following ways.

Quantity. Within three years after its establishment, CASC numbered sixty-five members—about half the non-regionally accredited colleges in the country. Total enrollment in the academic year of 1958–1959 was 30,581 students. Three colleges had fewer than 100 students; three had more than 2,000. The median was 312. As has already been pointed out, most of these colleges could double their enrollments in the next ten years. A few could triple their numbers. The total could easily be expanded toward 100,000 students at far less cost than would be required for a comparable expansion by starting new colleges or developing the expensive campuses of our large institutions.

The total value reported in plant and endowment was $71,934,314. During the fiscal year ending June 30, 1957, the last year for which figures are available, the individual member colleges raised $6,119,254 and CASC has raised $250,000 from corporations and foundations for the projects and operations of the council.

Quality. Although *quality* is far less susceptible of accurate measurement than *quantity,* at least some idea of these colleges can be gathered from the fact that membership in CASC implies being a four-year, degree-granting, private college of arts and sciences. It also implies approval by the state board of education or state university, or acceptance of credits by at least three regionally accredited institutions of higher education. Perhaps the most important qualification is that according to the CASC constitution a member must be "a college officially committed to, and presenting evidence of, an active program for early acceptance into the regional association." The whole program of the council has been geared to the aim of *advancing quality education.* The Fund for the Advancement of Education has given the greatest support to this program by three grants totaling $82,000 to underwrite a student-testing program conducted in part by the Educational Testing Service and in part by The Psychological Corporation; each test was followed up by a workshop. One reason for the testing program was to compare the performance of students in CASC colleges with those in other, fully accredited colleges. The results indicated a striking similarity between the two groups. One can say that the requirements for admission, promotion, and graduation in CASC colleges conform closely to the national pattern.

Variety. CASC members exhibit the "diversity and independence" which President Eisenhower termed characteristic of American higher education: forty are Protestant; sixteen are Catholic; nine are not church affiliated. Five of the group are Negro colleges. Fifty-three are coeducational; seven are for women only, and five are for men only. Every decade since the 1830s has seen the birth of at least one member. The oldest is McKendree—one hundred thirty years; the youngest is Chaminade College of Honolulu—four years. Some of these colleges are small, entirely residential but with students from every section of the country; some are larger, with only day or night students in attendance. Some are devoted completely to a liberal arts curriculum; others include a strong emphasis on a specialty, such as business, education, engineering, or religion.

Accessibility. CASC members may be found in thirty states from Maine to California. There are sixteen in New England and the Middle Atlantic States, thirty-two in the Middle West, eleven in the South, and six on the West Coast. Some are hidden in the mountains of Vermont and Kentucky; others front on the streets of Brooklyn, Hartford, and Detroit. They are accessible not only geographically but financially. The median cost to the student for board, room, tuition, and fees approximates $850.

Service Colleges

These colleges have been appropriately described as "service colleges" because sixty-one of the sixty-five offer programs in teacher education, fifty-six offer courses in religion, and forty-three include courses in business administration. This means that students can major in these subjects or receive degrees in these fields in addition to their work in the customary programs of liberal arts. Eighteen of these colleges recognize that many students need only a shorter period of education beyond the high school and offer a two-year terminal curriculum as well as the full four-year program. In several CASC colleges, a student can get a bachelor's degree in less than four years through summer study or an accelerated program.

Leadership

Leadership is important in the evaluation of a group. The sixty-five presidents of CASC colleges range in age from sixty-four to thirty years. The median age is fifty years. A third of the presidents hold earned doctor's degrees. Interestingly enough, the younger presidents in the newer colleges have had more professional training than their older colleagues in the older colleges. As a group, these institutions are led by presidents with many years of good service ahead of them. The leadership appears to be well balanced, with age and experience on the one hand and youth and professional training on the other.

THE IMPORTANCE OF SMALLNESS

Colleges, like people, form into groups or associations because of their mutual interests. The wide geographic distribution of the membership of CASC, the variety of types of control, the diversity of needs served by the different colleges are such as to make it surprising that this group ever found a common ground upon which to organize. The initial need which brought the members together was their common desire to break the vicious circle: no money without accreditation, no accreditation without money. However, it became apparent immediately that there were other and deeper interests. For example, there was a common desire to advance the quality of higher education by the improvement of academic programs far beyond the mere minimum standards required for accreditation. There was a common desire to obtain what Wilson Compton has called *national visibility* through collective action on a scale far beyond the means of any of the members individually. There was a common desire to help themselves, help each other, and receive help from professional consultants. No other existing organization (as has already been mentioned) was doing anything to serve the particular needs of these institutions; therefore, they banded together in true do-it-yourself style to help themselves.

However, there is one more essential point—size. In addition to its other purposes, CASC is the only association to serve as spokesman for a group of colleges because of their smallness. In a country which has become accustomed to thinking in terms of assembly-line production, bureaucracy, conformity, and huge organizations, it is no wonder that a group which publicized smallness as its greatest asset should attract attention.

That feature has inspired a mass of observations, and controversies. Do small colleges want to increase their enrollments in order to improve their finances? If so, won't they just become carbon copies of large colleges? Are small colleges efficient operating units? Wouldn't it be better for them to merge and become larger according to the pattern of big business? Do small colleges really have any justification for existence? Wouldn't they do better to become junior colleges and thereby join a growing national development in higher education? Is there any real virtue in smallness, or does smallness merely tend to perpetuate mediocre teaching on inferior campuses for students of limited academic ability? Can small colleges contribute anything worth while toward experimental education or will all the important experiments be conducted by larger institutions with great financial resources? And so it goes. The number and variety of questions are evidence of the genuine concern of thoughtful people over the role of the small college in America.

This subject of smallness was discussed informally but instructively on a radio program held in connection with the first CASC workshop at Nasson College in Maine during the summer of 1956. The moderator of the panel was Allen Jasper, representing station WWNH, Rochester, New Hampshire. The participants were William K. Selden, executive secretary of the National Commission on Accrediting, Royce S. Pitkin, president of Goddard College, Leymon W. Ketcham, assistant to the president of The King's College, and Roger C. Gay, president of Nasson College.

Edited Transcript of a Radio
Interview over Station WWNH covering the
Nasson Workshop in August, 1956

MR. JASPER: How do you define a small college?

DR. SELDEN: The word "small" is a relative term and what was considered small fifty or one hundred years ago is now not numerically the same size that you consider small. I would like to point out that there is a place in our society in this country for both the large universities and the small colleges and your workshop for the Council for the Advancement of Small Colleges to us in the National Commission on Accrediting is most encouraging and exceedingly gratifying because your emphasis has been placed upon improvements, advancement for them in order to do a better, a more quality type of job, and a better education. This is a desire which should be shared by all institutions.

MR. JASPER: Is there anything more to add to the definition of a small college?

DR. PITKIN: A small college, I would say, is an institution that is small enough to retain its position in the community. The average enrollment of the fifty colleges represented at this workshop is about three hundred students.

MR. JASPER: Is there really any advantage in the small college?

DR. PITKIN: Well, what a question to ask this group! You know, the amazing thing about the people in this workshop is that they are so filled with conviction that the small college has advantages that they just take it for granted. When nailed down, they really can come back to tell you why, too. One of the most important of these advantages is the sense of community. A small college is an institution that puts people together in a human relationship. You don't see part of the person in a small college, you work with the whole person. He isn't just a face that appears in front of you. He isn't a production unit that comes to your desk and gets marked by an automatic machine. He's an individual who says what he thinks to you and whom you can see. That is *the* great virtue of the small college.

MR. KETCHAM: I think we want to be perfectly honest and say, however, that most of us would like to be a little bit larger, although we are still in the category of the small college.

MR. JASPER: Not from the standpoint necessarily of having to have larger classes. You mean you'd like to be larger, I take it, in equipment, facilities, and what you can do for the student.

MR. KETCHAM: That's right.

DR. GAY: Now, I'll throw a question back to you, Mr. Jasper. Which would you prefer as a learning situation: a classroom in which you had a few fellow students and a good professor with whom you could have a natural interchange of opinion, and of whom you could ask questions, or a classroom with 3,600 students where you would be blatted at over a loud-speaker?

MR. JASPER: Well, you've asked a very good question because I happen to have been to both large colleges and small ones, and definitely I prefer the smaller, and I'm not saying that just because I'm in the present company either. Of course, I think that a student gets a feeling of belonging from the standpoint of the professor. The professor finds each student an individual and the student feels like an individual in a small college rather than just another product of a knowledge factory. I know in one or two of the large colleges I attended that I never did see the entire campus. I never did see all the buildings. I certainly didn't know one-tenth of the personnel. Whereas in a small college, I knew everybody from the top to the bottom, and I really enjoyed it much more.

DR. PITKIN: There is one other aspect of a small college that needs to be mentioned because of its importance and that is that the college is small enough so that it can be related to the community of which it is a part. Take Nasson here, for example, in Springvale. You know, Nasson is right on the street and it takes a lot of its educational program right out of the street. They have a merchandising program and it's built on what goes on in Springvale. It isn't something that goes on out in California where you sell oranges; it's up here where we sell lobsters. That's a tremendously important thing.

DR. GAY: Well, we had a choice a few years ago as to whether we wanted to stay on the main street of the town as we have or whether we wanted to go out in the country. We feel an education is a vital part of every community life. We like to feel that our college is just that sort of a part of the community, and we are staying on the main street, next to the stores, and we have a very healthy and wholesome interchange of opinion with all the merchants in our community, with all the people who live in our neighborhood. It is their college, we want them to feel that way, and I'm sure they do feel that way from the response we are getting.

MR. JASPER: I think that comes back to the fact that it is much more healthy for the college to be a part of the community than to get the feeling you sometimes do that this is an ivory tower of learning which is disassociated from everyday life. It is much more healthy when it is directly involved in daily life and the people in the town and the students themselves feel that. What should the general public realize about small colleges? What can they do to help solve the basic problems of these colleges?

MR. KETCHAM: I think the main thing for them to realize is the fact that if a college is small it does not indicate in the least that it is necessarily inferior in quality of its instruction. It is true we are hampered to a certain extent because of lack of funds and facilities, but in contrast to the mass production and the bigness and all the rest that goes with our thinking these days, we feel that if the American public should realize anew the importance of the small college in the total American scene and therefore support it and be interested in it and send their sons and daughters to it, this would be the biggest contribution they could possibly make.

MR. JASPER: Are there any other problems?

DR. PITKIN: Mr. Ketcham led right into this, really. The problems that these colleges face are connected with the problems faced by most colleges in this country. Any time you increase enrollment you have to take on new teachers; and every time you expand your plant you have to make readjustments in your educational program. Now we've been adding students throughout this country faster than we've been improving the quality of education, and in some cases the quality has actually deteriorated because we have lost track of the individual student. We tend to reach a point where we are handling too many students on a sort of a mass basis. You know, a kid in the back row has a certain number and he appears in the gradebook, but he is lost to the teacher as an individual. Our job here at this workshop is to find out how, even though these colleges get somewhat larger, they can retain the real advantage of person-to-person contact.

PIONEERING AND FLEXIBILITY

A good friend of CASC, Clarence H. Faust, president of the Fund for the Advancement of Education, delivered the main address at the council's first national meeting in January, 1957. On this occasion Dr. Faust said:

> As a group, the small colleges have a great opportunity to engage in the kind of pioneering that was earlier done in small colleges. Their first approach should be to solve the problems that the big institutions find it hard to solve. When an educational system becomes institutionalized, it is no longer flexible. Advancement does not come by way of systematization. It comes from new and urgent needs that have to be met. The small college is flexible enough to allow for experimentation, and the breakthrough in traditions is likely to come from the small college.

Here is the president of an influential foundation talking about flexibility, pioneering, experimentation, and departure from traditions. It is clear what he considers to be the role and the potential of the small college. His words acquire added significance in light of the fact that the Fund for the Advancement of Education has made a grant of $82,000 to CASC to conduct a student-testing program and to promote promising institutional experiments.

Perhaps one would not look for support of this position from the trustee of the educational fund of a large corporation, but here it is. The following statement was made by Arthur V. Wilker, trustee (retired) Union Carbide Educational Fund, at the Nasson Workshop in the summer of 1956:

> If I were a president or a member of the faculty of a small college, I certainly would stretch my imagination to the full extent in order to determine what I could do to make my college different and not perpetuate it as a smaller edition of the hundreds of larger ones already in existence.
>
> When one stops to think of the nine hundred and some regionally accredited colleges in the United States, one is almost appalled by the fact that, in an overwhelming majority of cases by class, one is just like another.

This statement should be underlined by the fact that Union Carbide was the first large corporation to support CASC with a grant of $26,500—$500 apiece to each of its then fifty-three members.

EXPERIMENT OR CONFORMITY

William G. Land, "an independent investigator specializing in educational and manpower problems," has expressed his opinion in the *Journal of Higher Education*:[1]

> If small colleges are to advance their educational standards and at the same time remain financially stable, they will have to experiment. They cannot merely ape their larger and more affluent brethren and achieve the same results.
>
> [Mr. Land notes that] in a sense the history of progress can be defined as essentially the history of heresy.

[1] William G. Land, "Experiment or Conformity in the Small College?" *Journal of Higher Education*, June, 1957.

Then he calls for "heresy" in a number of areas: admissions policies, cooperative use of libraries, sharing of academic and administrative talent, methods of instruction, and development of curriculum:

> All this cannot be done by conforming to the normal path of academic operation. It will require experiment, imagination, and at least a minor amount of heresy. . . . If liberal education in the small college is to hold its own and contribute . . . to the nation's supply of intellectually able manpower and woman power, we need more heresy to confound the orthodox. If practical training in operations and techniques is to meet the nation's need for competent workers, we need continued experimentation to combat complacency. Small colleges have an important place in American education. In competition with the mass production of undergraduates they hold enormous potential for molding and maturing the products of a quality education. The advancement of small colleges is more than a matter of maintaining their existence: it is a challenge to support educational integrity.

THE UNIQUE SERVICE OF THE SMALL COLLEGE

The comments reported so far have been made by a foundation president, a corporation trustee, and an independent observer. It might be interesting to get a close-up of the small colleges through the eyes of one of their presidents.

The following observations on the role of the small college were made by Roger C. Gay, president of Nasson College, Springvale, Maine. He was addressing a meeting keyed to the theme, *new patterns in higher education.* His subject was "The Unique Service of the Small College." [2]

> The idea of applying assembly-line technique to the education of human beings is appalling to a great many of us. It represents one of the final steps in turning out an endless procession of "gray flannel minds" for unimaginative existence in a

[2] Roger C. Gay, address before the Conference on New Colleges for a New Day, in the series "Great Ideas in Higher Education," sponsored by Goddard College, New York City, Jan. 18, 1958.

completely homogenized society. Without any doubt, professors in great universities feel concern for the individual, but what chance does the professor have to carry this into action in a class where as many as 1,500 students may be hearing a lecture over loud-speakers? How much can the student expect at a middle western university where graduate students and even senior students must help to carry the teaching load? For myself, I would much rather study at *Littleknown College* under *Professor Anonymous* who uses *Professor Greatman's* text, than listen with 1,500 others at the university to *Professor Greatman's* lecture over a public address system supplemented by a weekly discussion group led by an overworked graduate student a couple of years older than myself, who may very well feel his weekly chore is an undesirable means towards the end of continuing on at graduate school.

Small colleges have long been considered the seed beds for educational experimentation—for the development of new ideas and approaches in education. Anyone who has tried to buck an idea through the departmental organization and on up through the university senate knows what a frustrating experience it can be to try to change anything. I know that I have seen enough of it to wed me everlastingly to the small college. Run down the list of colleges for yourselves and consider where the real pioneering goes on. The list ranges alphabetically from Antioch, Bard, Bennington, Goddard, through Nasson, Reed, Sarah Lawrence, and Swarthmore, clear down to William Penn and Yankton. All down the list you will find small colleges experimenting, undergoing critical self-appraisal, and improving, because with relative smallness there is a high degree of flexibility and responsiveness to changing needs and conditions. In my own institution, Nasson, for example, we are experimenting among other things with the integration of professionally oriented subject matter with the traditional liberal arts.

President Eisenhower, former President Truman, President Pusey of Harvard, and a great many others have in various ways spelled out the need for a union of professional and liberal education. Yet, how much actual experimentation is going on in this area beyond a reshuffling of existing courses? With some thirty faculty members, it is a fairly simple matter to effect an integrated approach to a particular problem (and this is as often as not accomplished over the coffee cups in the corner shop or the faculty lounge). It is much easier in a small college than it is in a large university for members of one department to get together with those in another. By way of illustration of how complete this process of isolation can be, there was a story in the paper recently of two cousins who had completely lost track of each other over the years being reunited when both were being honored for twenty-five years of service in the same institution.

The list of special advantages which contributes to the unique service of the small college is still not complete. However, I should like to direct your attention to one aspect which perhaps, above all others, is unique in these institutions, and responsible for the success of their graduates. Because of the relatively small numbers of people involved, a sense of identification with the whole group is almost unavoidable.

In the small college, individuals of diverse abilities, interests, and backgrounds are constantly thrown together with unequaled opportunity for the exchange of ideas. There is little chance for them to become encapsulated in little homogeneous groups or cliques. The result for the individual is generally a healthy adjustment to the problems of modern social interaction, avoiding the extremes of militant individualism and rigid conformity. Opportunities for participation in extracurricular or co-curricular activities, in student government, even in educational and social policy determination, differ among colleges, but the opportunities for this experience are far more available to each student in the smaller institutions. We hear a great deal, currently, of the value of group dynamics, and all sorts of pedagogic devices are suggested to provide a medium for this process. On the small college campus there is a constant natural environment for group dynamics which should be far more productive than any artificially contrived situation. Again, the end product is the best yardstick. There are several studies which show that the alumni of small colleges are much more active in their local communities than those of larger institutions.

These, then, are some rather general reflections on the unique service of the small college in meeting the needs for new colleges for a new day. If these needs are to be met, colleges must, to the best of their ability, be responsive to change—be attuned to the dynamics of evolution and development. It is not enough to arrange for a student to be hit on the head by a falling apple and tortuously retrace Newton's reasoning on gravity. No matter how successful he may be in recreating within himself an identification with Newton in his great step beyond the seventeenth century, until he can apply these practices and principles to contemporary problems, knowledge of the past is of little value except as it relates to the present and future.

The solution of the problems of the new day calls for the utmost in creative thinking by dynamic individuals. No discoveries were ever made by those who travel only on the numbered highways. The small colleges are doing an excellent job of developing men and women who are equipped and eager to strike out for themselves. As in the past, the bright hope of the future lies in a plentiful supply of educated people who can deal confidently and constructively with the unknown. This is the greatest contribution which the small colleges can make.

THE PROFESSOR'S VIEWPOINT

Elton Trueblood, a distinguished professor in a well-known small college, had this to say in the *Reader's Digest* of September, 1956.

> The professor in the small school may not have all the fancy equipment he wishes he had. But one thing he has: students in numbers small enough so that each, for him, is a person in whose present and future welfare he can take an intimate interest.

In this same article he cited several other authorities as follows:

> A careful research project conducted by Professors Robert H. Knapp and H. B. Goodrich of Wesleyan University shows, for instance, that "small liberal arts colleges are far and away the most productive sources of future scientists." Of the first fifty institutions in America, judged by the scientific eminence of their graduates, thirty-nine are small, privately supported colleges.
>
> There is like evidence that the small independent college—out of all proportion to the number of its students or its material resources—produces eminence in the economic life of our nation. A recent study of 33,500 business executives shows that 88 per

cent are college graduates, and of that number 71 per cent come from generally small liberal arts schools.

At the end of 1952 there were reported to be sixty-six billion-dollar corporations in the United States. Of the 106 board chairmen and presidents of these business giants, 66—that is 62.3 per cent—were graduates of such independent institutions. Roger M. Blough, chairman of the U.S. Steel Corp., for example, is a graduate of Susquehanna University; Eugene G. Grace, chairman of the Bethlehem Steel Corp., of Lehigh University; Harlow H. Curtice, president of General Motors, of Ferris Institute; Robert E. Wilson, chairman of the Standard Oil Co. of Indiana, of Wooster College; Ralph J. Cordiner, president of General Electric, of Whitman College; John J. McCloy, chairman of the Chase-Manhattan Bank, of Amherst College.

As for leaders in the humanistic fields, Lynn White, Jr., president of Mills College, has said, "There is every reason to believe small colleges give intellectual birth to at least as high a proportion of them as of natural scientists." Support for this is found in a survey made by the editors of *Who's Who in America,* which showed that "small schools, in relation to their enrollment, contributed the highest percentage" of those who merit rating in that catalogue of distinction.

The publication, *The Younger American Scholars,* by Knapp and Greenbaum adds some further interesting light.[3] Of those institutions producing the greatest percentage of scholars, six of the first ten are definitely small colleges. Only one state university appears in the first thirty. Swarthmore heads the list with a score of 61.2 per 1,000, compared with Harvard's 27.3 per 1,000.

PANEL ON SMALL COLLEGES

In order to round out the picture which appears to be in the public mind regarding small colleges, I shall quote a number of excerpts from a panel discussion held at Miami Beach on Jan-

[3] R. H. Knapp and J. J. Greenbaum, *The Younger American Scholars,* University of Chicago Press: Chicago, 1953. Published for Wesleyan University, Middletown, Conn.

uary 6, 1958. The occasion was the second national meeting of CASC. The theme was *How the Small College Meets the Challenge.* The speakers were Philip E. Jacob, professor of political science at the University of Pennsylvania and author of *Changing Values in College*; Paul Woodring, consultant to the Fund for the Advancement of Education and author of *A Fourth of a Nation;* Harold Taylor, then president of Sarah Lawrence College, author of *On Education and Freedom*; and Kenneth G. Patrick, then manager of educational relations and corporate support services of the General Electric Company—a recognized leader in the field of college and industry relations. The moderator of the panel was Herman R. Allen, education editor of *Newsweek.*

Dr. Taylor expressed his concern over the current intellectual flabbiness and complacency of our American culture. He felt that at the root of this situation were large institutions where students often regarded clothes, cars, fraternities, and other symbols of social success as more important than the development of their intellects and talents. He took an unusual viewpoint:

> . . . the small unaccredited college is the luckiest college in the United States right now. You are lucky because you're broke and unaccredited. When you are broke and unaccredited, you are most likely to live by your wits and not be complacent, the way most of higher education in America has been and is. . . . If you are not accredited, you are released from the inhibitions of trying to be respectable and be like every other institution in the country. . . . I think, on the other hand, that if you want to be valuable to American education now, you will become extraordinarily adventurous because you have nothing to lose. You will remain broke and unaccredited unless you have something terribly important to give to America.

Dr. Woodring picked up the suggestions made by Dr. Taylor with the following comments:

> There is a need for true experimentation in higher education. Go back in the twenties and thirties and try to think of the names of the experimental colleges in that era; you can name certainly

half a dozen, probably more of the truly experimental colleges. Look around the country today for their equivalents and the number will be much smaller. You may have trouble finding any that are truly experimental. Now why this is, I really don't know—whether it's in the nature of the cultural trend itself or what. Colleges like your own are probably in a dilemma here which I recognize, and I don't know how to tell you to get out of it. But in your efforts to become accredited, you are likely to imitate accredited colleges, and this, I think, would be fatal. I think you could find better ways of doing things. I would hope the accrediting agencies would have imagination enough to accept you, or maybe you are able to develop strength enough to ignore the accrediting agencies—one or the other. It is quite possible that the accrediting agencies will recognize this. We do need true experimentation.

As an experiment, I would like to see some college try to see if it couldn't develop the smallest catalogue in the country—two pages, oh, I'd allow it to go up to ten—but the tendency of small colleges has been to try to develop catalogues as big as the big colleges. This means that the curriculum is as large. This means in many small colleges that a teacher whose education has been specialized in one area has to teach in four or five areas, and then he teaches some other things on the side for which he is totally unqualified. By simplifying the curriculum you could make the faculty much more useful, probably have a much better curriculum. This means, of course, giving up the smorgasbord or cafeteria type of curriculum. This means the faculty would have to make some decisions about the broad areas of knowledge that are essential. While this is difficult for the faculty to do, it's even harder for the student. It seems to me unwise to ask a student to choose among courses in epistemology, ichthyology, and anthropology when he doesn't even know what any of them mean. He can't. It's like asking a blind man to state his favorite color. But some decisions have to be made, and if you are willing to make these, you can greatly simplify the curriculum. This means, of course, that the college will have to know where it's going, and I would venture a guess that if you go around the colleges represented here, almost every college has three or four, or at least a couple, of outstanding teachers. Your problem is to hold these at all costs. This probably means that you ought to throw away all salary schedules, if you have any. You ought to hold these people. For, if you lose these, you're not going to be able to replace them on the coming market. If you have distinguished older people, you can probably hold them because they have a feeling of commitment. But it is essential that you hold them. As I think about the four or five small colleges with which I have been associated as student and teacher, it seems to me that in every one there are a few of these outstanding people. Now they're not necessarily famous: some of them have never written —neither did Socrates ever write anything. But they're the outstanding teachers, and it's the job of the administrator to recognize these people and somehow to give them whatever it takes to hold them. This is not primarily financial, but it probably includes some money.

Now if you can do these things: make a small catalogue and keep your curriculum simple, I think your money would stretch a good deal farther than if you try to offer a great deal. This means that you do not offer much diversity. It is essential that American higher education should be characterized by diversity, but this does not mean that every institution needs to be characterized by great diversity. A student chooses a certain kind of curriculum when he chooses a college. When he goes to M.I.T., he decides on a career in a kind of curriculum. If he goes to a medical school, he makes a choice. It seems reasonable that the college ought to grow on its own strength. In a small college, this means that you will have to build curriculum in part around the faculty. If you have two or three outstanding people in literature, let that be the core of your curriculum. But in any case, it means that your college should not try to diversify, should not try to imitate the large college. That seems to me to be a prominent ailment of small colleges. They try to act like large colleges or universities, and you can read this in their catalogues —that they try to do more than they can. But if they could simplify the curriculum, keep the catalogue small, take pride in the things they don't offer, then I should think their contribution would be very great.

Mr. Patrick approached the problem of the small college from the viewpoint of industry with the interesting observation that the General Electric Company with 185,000 employees included about 20,000 college graduates—a ratio of about 1 to 9. "The thing which surprised a good many of my associates," he said, "was the fact that over one-third of these had been generally educated and not technically educated."

Mr. Patrick emphasized the point that business was extremely liberal with regard to its support of education without demanding any *quid pro quo*. However, he did point out that when the small colleges were talking about raising 3 million dollars for faculty salaries, it meant the 5 per cent profit factor on 6 million dollars' worth of sales; when Mr. Hoover mentioned 75 million dollars as the sum needed to put all these colleges on their feet, he was talking about the profit on 1.5 billion dollars in sales, and when the figure of 6 hundred million dollars for education had been cited for the previous year, it was the profit on 12 billion dollars' worth of sales. "Not all of this is business given," he said, "but I contend that all of it is business produced, for personally I know of no other way to get these dollars except out of the economy. . . . These are all business dollars; they are no different from any other kind."

Dr. Jacob looked at the potentiality of the small college somewhat wistfully from the standpoint of a professor in a large university:

> May I put in a plug for a different dimension of education than that which has been covered so far? It seems to me that one of the reasons for the hiatus which apparently exists between our academic program and student values is that we really never come to grips with the student's own experiences. He is really introduced into an ivory tower classroom. I would just like to say that it seems to me that the smaller colleges represented here with their close ties with communities are in an unusually favorable position to cultivate experience-oriented education—one in which the classroom and the community are alike parts of the educational program. The curriculum may be consciously inclusive of experiences that will be meaningful in a student's own eyes in terms of the decisions that he has to make and will expect to make in the course of the succeeding years. I have a feeling that we are too academic in the accredited colleges. Speaking as a teacher from one of them, it is extremely difficult to design experience-oriented education at the University of Pennsylvania

in a city of 3 million. Perhaps these colleges which you represent could think of ways in which the education a student gets is a living education—an education in the student's own terms of life.

DIFFERENCES IN VIEWPOINT

There is an old story about three men standing on the north rim of the Grand Canyon. The first was a minister, the second an artist, and the third a farmer.

As the minister gazed into the canyon, he was impressed by the scene and he said, "What a magnificent testimony this is to the power of the Almighty. How insignificant is the power of man in comparison with the divine force which could produce such a phenomenon."

As the artist gazed into the canyon, he, too, was impressed by its grandeur. "Oh, if only I had the skill with eye and hand," he said, "to capture the beauty of this scene and record it for posterity."

When the farmer gazed into the canyon, he was no less impressed than his two companions. He spat over the edge and listened attentively. Finally, he said, "What a hell of a place to lose a cow."

It is much the same way with observers of the small college. One could easily imagine such reactions as the following:

STUDENT: What a wonderful opportunity this small college presents for me to make friends, participate in student activities, become intimately acquainted with scholarly professors, and enjoy an informal life in pleasant surroundings for four years.

PROFESSOR: Here is just what I have been looking for all my life—a small college with a chance to know my students as individuals, a place where my teaching will be appreciated and I will not have to write books, make speeches, and engage in obscure research in order to be promoted.

PRESIDENT: The small college is the place for me. I'd rather be a big frog in a small puddle than a small frog in a big puddle. No red tape—I can get things done. Quality, not quantity—the small college gives me a chance to strike a blow for excellence rather than mediocrity.

PROFESSOR OF EDUCATION: Ah, ha! Here it is—the small college. This is the place to experiment with new courses, teaching methods, testing programs, and reorganization of the curriculum. There is a good chance to do something new and interesting in the small college unfettered by traditions, unhampered by considerations of status, relatively free from vested interests, and elaborate academic machinery.

CORPORATION EXECUTIVE: Economy—that's the answer. The small college can stretch a dollar further in terms of plant and personnel than is possible in the large college or the public institution. Here is a chance to develop an untapped resource in the same way I would build up a small manufacturing plant to meet a new demand. Free enterprise—the small college is the place to train the future leaders of business and industry. Here is a chance for the *big* to help the *small* in true American fashion.

FOUNDATION EXECUTIVE: The small college is very different from the large university—*vive la différence!* The small college is the seed bed of great ideas. It is the last remaining place in our society where an individual can be himself without undue concern about conformity. It deserves support.

GROUP IMPACT

The importance of the group as a whole is far more impressive than that of any one college in particular. It is interesting to note that there is a small Catholic college on the banks of the Rio Grande where the good sisters are living missionary lives in the service of the Mexicans and the Indians. But this one college will probably not be the salvation of the Christian tradition in a wicked world. It is rather inspiring to discover a small college in the hills of Vermont dedicated to educational experiment to such a degree that it is willing to depart from traditional entrance requirements, customary practices regarding class attendance, the accepted use of examinations, even the traditional ceremonies at commencement. But this one college is not likely to revolutionize higher education in America.

It is impressive to discover a college in the Southern mountains serving a group of boys and girls who would have little chance of any education beyond the offering of a mediocre high school were it not for the dedicated service of this institution. But it is most unlikely that this one college will be turning out future Abraham Lincolns in sufficient quantity to influence the trend of major events.

The important thing—the great potential—is that we now have an organized group of sixty-five small colleges in thirty states stretching all the way from the eastern border of Maine to the coast of Oregon. The variety within this group is enormous. Here is the chance to preserve tradition, if that is our inclination. Here is the chance to promote the ideals of Christian education through sixteen Catholic colleges and fourteen different kinds of Protestant colleges. Here is the chance to emphasize the diversity of our American culture by strengthening the service which these colleges individually perform in their own communities and regions. Here is the chance to experiment with all the revolutionary ideas we want in a group which is receptive to new ideas and will give them an open-minded and sympathetic criticism.

These colleges enrolled 30,581 students in 1958–1959; their combined assets approximated 72 million dollars. This constitutes a far greater national asset than if the same totals were sliced three ways into three institutions of 10,000 students each. If that were done, we would have three college presidents instead of sixty-five; we would be serving three areas instead of sixty-five; we would be draining away both brains and dollars from sixty-five communities and centralizing them in three. We would at best be representing three different educational philosophies instead of many times that number. We would be heading in the direction of more conformity rather than more diversity; we would have taken a lot of the salt and pepper out of the educational stew, leaving it flat and tasteless.

The small size of each unit, the large number of units and their scattered geographic distribution, the tremendous variety of needs being served through the efforts of many small leaders rather than a few giants, all constitute the unique feature of this group as a whole. Here is where the national opportunity lies—to strengthen the group as a whole and the individuals within the group so that they may better perform their functions whatever they are and better serve their clientele whoever they may be.

Money, consultant service, official recognition, genuine encouragement from the educational profession, from foundations, from corporations, and from the public are needed in order to help these colleges help themselves along the road of greater service to the country.

This is the group potential of the small colleges. This is how the small colleges can meet the challenge of diversity and independence in American education.

Chapter 3

SOUL SEARCHING

How can the small colleges meet the challenge of improving educational programs and experimenting with new ideas? In other words, how can they fulfill the potentialities ascribed to them by financial and educational leaders?

WORKSHOPS

One way is to hold workshops or conferences for the exchange of ideas and information and for the benefits to be derived from a joint attack upon common problems.

At the time of this writing (spring, 1959) CASC has held four such workshops.

Nasson Workshop. The first workshop was held in August, 1956, on the campus of Nasson College in Springvale, Maine. The theme of this meeting was *What Should a Small Liberal Arts College Be?* This broad topic was divided into four subtopics: (1) curriculum, (2) teaching methods, (3) management, and

(4) development programs. At this meeting, forty-nine colleges were represented from twenty-five states. President Royce S. Pitkin of Goddard College served as program director.

Milligan Workshop. The second workshop was held at Milligan College in Tennessee in August, 1957. In the spring of 1957, the Fund for the Advancement of Education gave CASC a grant of $56,000 to finance the administration of the area tests of the Graduate Record Examinations to 2,450 sophomores and 1,723 seniors in fifty-two colleges. This was followed by a grant of $15,000 to meet the costs of the Milligan Workshop, to study the results of the tests, and to relate them to programs of improvement and experiment on individual campuses. The theme of this meeting was *Improving Our Educational Program.*

Its purposes were (1) to study ways by which the greatest value could be derived from the council's testing program, (2) to relate the use of tests to evaluation of the teaching-learning conditions in the member colleges, (3) to consider ways by which the educational programs of colleges could be further improved, and (4) to consider the possibilities for experimentation within each college. The director of the workshop was Dr. Ralph W. Tyler, director of the Center for Advanced Study in the Behavioral Sciences, Palo Alto, California. A consultant was Charles R. Langmuir, director of special projects, The Psychological Corporation, New York. This meeting was attended by 120 persons representing 60 member colleges.

Goddard Mid-winter Conference. The third workshop was called the Mid-winter Conference and was held on the campus of Goddard College, Vermont, for three days in February, 1958. It was financed by a grant of $11,000 from the Fund for the Advancement of Education. The purposes were (1) to report and evaluate progress made in carrying out the plans for educational advancement developed at the summer workshop, (2) to study, with a view to action, proposals for educational experimentation made at the Milligan Workshop and to consider any others that may emerge from the conference, and (3) to examine the results of the council's fall testing program and to consider their implications for improvement or modification of educational programs of the individual colleges. The director was Samuel B. Gould, then president of Antioch College. There were forty-eight colleges represented from twenty-six states. Among those present were twenty-five presidents, twenty-four deans, and several faculty members.

Michigan Workshop. A fourth workshop took place in August, 1958, on the campus of Michigan State University. It continued the academic study already started in the three earlier meetings and added an examination of the business-management practices of the member colleges. The unique feature of this workshop was that it brought together the three top administrators of each college (president, dean, and business manager) for a joint consideration of the problems of academic and financial management.

WORKSHOP REVIEW

It should be clear from the description of these four workshops that CASC has been consistently carrying out a program of *advancing quality education* according to its stated purpose. It is appropriate to review these workshops in order to see what ideas were expressed and to report on improvements and experiments in progress. In order to do this, the workshops will be considered not chronologically but topically so that the important ideas can be presented under three headings: (1) *criticisms,* (2) *questions raised,* and (3) *observations, advice,* and *inspiration.* This discussion will be followed by a review of the results of the testing program and an analysis of the experimental programs in progress.

Criticisms

Small colleges have been criticized recently as marginal operations both educationally and financially. This would seem to apply to colleges with fewer than 1,000 students—which would mean two-thirds of those in the country and almost all those represented at the meeting.

On the other hand, it has been said that higher education

suffers from giantism. Size, mass, and poundage, the laby-rinthine, many-storied buildings, the herded thousands of students and staff make most of the evils of modern college life inevitable. Size necessitates organization, and we have a tendency to organize the enjoyment out of learning in large institutions.

Higher education has been accused of prolonging the adolescence of college youth by denying them the opportunities to carry adult responsibilities as soon as possible. It has also been accused of keeping students in a social vacuum by isolating them on campuses divorced from any true relationships with their local communities.

Many colleges—particularly small ones—have been criticized for overloading their curricula with too many courses, for trying to be all things to all people, and for publishing catalogues which were fantastically full and complicated.

College teachers have been criticized for being specialists in subject matter rather than in teaching and for attempting to be mere purveyors of information rather than agents of change in student behavior.

Small colleges have been criticized on the basis that a one-man department was too limited to provide an adequate educational offering. Similarly it has been pointed out that small colleges with limited library and laboratory facilities were at a great disadvantage. However, these limitations, it was found, could be turned to advantage if resourceful teachers found ways of improving and expanding the opportunities for learning by greater use of their surrounding communities and sometimes by pooling their resources with neighboring colleges.

Boards of trustees have come under attack for being too complacent in their attitude and not shouldering real responsibility for the progress of the college.

Small colleges have been criticized for not organizing and cultivating their own alumni for financial support.

From the standpoint of business management, small colleges have been urged to raise their sights, be more alert to their opportunities for economy and efficiency, and to make a positive rather than a negative approach to their administrative problems.

Questions Raised

1. Should small colleges grow bigger simply for the sake of size? What are the true strengths and weaknesses of small colleges? What should a small liberal arts college really be?

2. One fundamental and important series of questions was this: what is the true purpose of the council? What *can* it do? What *should* it do?

It appears to me [states President Pitkin] that the main function of this organization is public relations—both external and internal. If we are going to present our case to the public, we have to know what it is we're going to say. We must ask ourselves frankly about the strengths and weaknesses represented in this group. Why should a philanthropist or an industrialist or foundation executive give anything to any one of us in preference to any one of a hundred other institutions? One of the most important considerations in giving is not altruism but prestige to the donor. What kind of case can we present? If we haven't anything more than sentiment on the part of our alumni, our appeal is pretty limited. If a group of impartial observers who knew something about education were to look at our colleges, would they say, "You'd better give your money to the colleges in CASC rather than to Harvard or Amherst, or the University of California"? You see, we have to look pretty hard to find what we have to offer that is superior. Are there in this group, ten colleges with distinctive programs to be presented to a foundation? Are there any that are doing new things that are faster, cheaper, or better than what is already going on in higher education? What would we do with additional money that we cannot do now? How would we improve our academic programs or physical plants? How can we justify our appeal for support? I have an idea that if we, as a council, could find as few as ten members each of which was doing something really unique and experimental we'd be made. We'd get support and acceptance. But whether we set out to be different or not, we still have to be good. We have to have something really good for the public to look at, not just pretty girls or impressive buildings.

This line of questioning and answering led to a similar question from a different point of view and to a different answer.

3. "What's your rallying cry?" asked Wade Arnold, president of Affiliated Public Relations, Inc. "What's your special character? What are the words that make sense for *you?*" Then he asked a really heart-warming rhetorical question:

> Where in America today can a man or woman get a better general education than in the small college of liberal arts? Where is the spirit of free inquiry, the divine impulse to question and explore, the sense of humble obligation to doubt it until you prove it, more alive than in the small college of liberal arts?

Mr. Arnold answered several of his own questions with this challenging statement:

> If liberty was the spirit of the eighteenth century, and industrialization of the nineteenth, perhaps the trend of the twentieth is toward conformity. In this jungle of pressures to make us all dress alike and look alike and think alike and act alike, the small college is a ray of light, a reminder that teachers in communion with students are more important than buildings. The finest laboratory in the world is nothing but a dead weight of chrome and glass in the absence of an eager and inquiring mind. People who think for themselves are more important than things.

4. Two questions were asked of William K. Selden, executive secretary of the National Commission on Accrediting. First, "What are the requirements of the regional associations and are they changing?"

He answered that although the requirements were somewhat different in the six associations there was a definite shift in emphasis away from judging an institution by quantitative criteria in favor of judgments based on qualitative criteria. This was very encouraging to a number of CASC presidents and led logically to the second question, "What can a college do to improve its program that does not require money?"

Mr. Selden's answer was not what might be expected—reorganization of the curriculum, improvement of instruction in a particular subject, or reappraisal of institutional objectives.

Instead he said, "The first thing a college ought to do is to give attention to the administrative end of the institution. There are many things an institution can do when there is an alert president at the head of it."

Mr. Selden went on to point out that accreditation was not intended to be a strait jacket, to prevent worthwhile experiment, to exaggerate the importance of conformity. It was intended to stimulate improvement and growth. He felt that great benefit could come to the member institutions from their association in CASC because of their coordinated efforts at improvement and the stimulation to be derived from workshops, national meetings, consultant services, and self-studies. Subsequent events have proved this opinion to be correct.

5. Another series of questions had to do with management problems. "Could we, as a council, make a study of per student costs? A great deal is said about inefficiency in small colleges. However, there is some evidence to the contrary—that costs are actually less in small colleges. If we could demonstrate this, and show it is for valid reasons of economy, not just underpaying the faculty, we'd have an important story to tell."

6. An estimate was made that the members of the council needed as many as twenty-eight new buildings. Would a careful study of the situation support this estimate or would we find we had unused community resources available? For example, Hillyer College is using the laboratory facilities of a nearby hospital for teaching a particular branch of science. This is a resource with tremendously expensive equipment that the college never had to pay for. Could we not do the same thing in a rural college by using the laboratory of nature for teaching biology? Could we not do the same thing again by using our local communities as living laboratories for the study of sociology?

Are there ways in which we could utilize our plants to greater advantage by holding summer sessions or night classes? No manufacturing company could stay in business with its plant closed down three months of the year or a great deal of its space lying idle a large part of each day. Why should colleges be any different?

At the Goddard Mid-winter Conference, H. Harry Giles, professor of education, New York University, raised a series of questions related to the potentiality of the small college in the field of experimentation. He is quoted as follows.

How do you select the objectives of your educational experimentation? I hope that as presidents you will select these objectives by asking the right questions rather than by telling people. I hope you will do it by testing rather than demanding, by encouraging, and by a great awareness of what is possible. I think one of the reasons why these meetings are important to us is to get a picture of the whole range of possibilities that can be shown by members of the group.

I think that these are some of the issues in American education which perhaps you as leaders of small colleges in America in this day are contributing to and can contribute to.

1. Whether subject-matter content is an end in itself or a tool to be used in living and thinking?

2. Whether teaching should be forcible feeding or the creation of conditions for self-teaching?

3. How many subjects can a student master in a given time and how many of the subjects should be required, and on what basis should elective subjects be offered?

4. What do social relationships have to do with learning and democratic citizenship?

5. To what extent should all classroom teaching pay heed to what should be done by the whole group, and pay heed equally to what should be done by special interest and ability groups, and equally to what should be done by individuals?

6. If some say the only road to success is fragmentation and if we say, no, we must have integration, first, what has been attempted in this line, and second, what remains for us to discover about how to go at it?

7. Should there be self-government, self-discipline, or authority and imposed regulations in student life?

8. What is the function of the lecture, if any, and what is the function of discussion, if any?

9. What kinds of self-evaluation should every student and every faculty member and every administrator learn? What kinds

of external evaluation by others should be applied, and should any evaluation be punitive?

10. What kind of social philosophy do our students have and what kinds of learnings do they need about the direction of our society in this age of technology?

11. What economic forces are likely most to affect the lives and development of our students and how much do they understand these forces? Not many here remember that in the Depression men killed themselves because they didn't know that they were in the grip of economic forces beyond their powers of control; they still thought it was true that if they were any good they could earn a living.

12. To what extent are the arts and the whole nature of creativity in man of first importance in all education, and how do you feed this human need?

13. The same with the sciences.

14. To what extent should we use the study of the community around us as one of our greatest resources in education?

15. What services should the college, its faculty, and its students offer to its community?

16. With what prejudices, what attitudes, what stereotypes, and hence, what limitations of perceptions do students come to us, and do we increase or decrease the blinding effect of preconception?

17. How are vocational choices influenced by the types of education we have provided?

18. What knowledge of health and recreation—*mens sana in corpore sano,* the old idea—how much attention do we pay to it?

19. Are we constantly experimenting with educational procedures, and if so, in what way?

20. With what motivations and expectations do new students come to college, do teachers come to college, do administrators come to college?

Observations, Advice, and Inspiration

The criticisms which were cited and the questions which were raised and discussed naturally stimulated a number of constructive statements. A few of these are paraphrased in order to indicate promising lines of future development for small colleges in general and for the members of CASC as a group to follow.

Karl W. Bigelow, professor of education, Teachers College, Columbia, told the Nasson conference:

> The surest way to attract financial support is to have a superior educational program, curriculum, and teachers; plenty of money is no guarantee of a superior program unless there are also people with ideas, imagination, courage, dedication, zest, and a willingness to experiment. . . . A very important administrative function is to select and encourage creative people. Learning will improve as soon as the curriculum is made realistic in terms of student needs and interests. The four keys to success in improvement of college teaching are experimentation, freedom, realism, and scholarship.

David M. Church, executive director of the American Association of Fund-Raising Counsel said,

> There are many successful men and women today who remember that some of the finest teaching they had, came not in the lecture halls presided over by great teachers, but in the classrooms, from good teachers who had not yet risen above the instructor's level. . . . Sound management is of the utmost importance. . . . Success in a fund-raising campaign will require unanimous agreement at the top level. . . . I see no reason why the citizens of a community should not contribute annually to their college as they do to their community chest. . . . It may be that small colleges have a case to present in the sound education they offer in an atmosphere of normalcy rather than one of constant intellectual competition.

Wilson M. Compton, former president of the Council for Financial Aid to Education, told CASC:

> Corporate giving has achieved a new record as a source of support for higher education. . . . The small colleges have the means of doing two things which are very precious—first, the treatment of the individual student as an individual—second, an opportunity to maintain the religious and spiritual element in American life.

Theodore A. Distler, executive director of the Association of American Colleges, said,

> It is better and more economical to conserve and build on our present resources than to start something entirely new. Small colleges should search their souls clearly and objectively with respect to aims, functions, and performance. Unless they are willing to do this honestly, and act on the basis of an objective assessment they have no right to ask for financial support, and should close up. . . . Some should merge, some should change their function, some should change their program. . . . All of them should make sure they have used their natural constituencies —alumni, friends, trustees, and community—before asking corporations, or foundations for financial support.

John M. Schlegel, treasurer of Lafayette College, told CASC members:

> Each college need not be self-contained. . . . Cooperation between colleges is encouraged. . . . Facilities, faculty, and equipment offer possibilities for intercollege cooperation. . . . This also applies to library and laboratory facilities, and purchasing. . . . Your challenge as a leader is to use your opportunity to raise your sights on a second-mile accomplishment, which calls for creative thinking, planning, and alertness to new trends. . . . Today you ought to be doing all you can to get your buildings in shape to this dollar's worth, because five years from now today's dollar will be worth only 80 cents.

William K. Selden, executive secretary of the National Commission on Accrediting, made this observation:

> An institution which is not now devoting a high proportion of its income to instructional activities is likely to find itself in a condition which will grow steadily worse in the coming years. . . . Colleges of fewer than five or six hundred students are likely to operate at a disadvantage in terms of efficiency, as well as in stimulation of academic programs.

Ernest T. Stewart, Jr., executive director of the American Alumni Council, made this statement:

A college has at least three responsibilities toward its alumni: (1) to initiate and maintain a well-rounded program, (2) to subsidize the program in part, or completely, (3) regardless of subsidization, to maintain the fiction of alumni independence.

A. V. Wilker, former trustee of the Union Carbide Educational Fund, expressed this view,

> It would seem to me that the smaller colleges have within the limits of their resources greater possibilities for the exceptional handling of the exceptional scholar than do the larger universities.
>
> If I were a president or a member of the faculty of a small college, I certainly would stretch my imagination to the fullest extent in order to determine what I could do to make my college different and not perpetuate it as a small edition of the hundreds of the larger already in existence.
>
> *You men of the smaller colleges and universities represent the seed beds of higher education. It is logical to assume that the future growth of private higher education in this country is dependent upon your survival.*

Royce S. Pitkin, president of Goddard College, regarded CASC in this light:

> The council must be a service group, and not a pressure group. It is not our purpose to put pressure upon regional associations for accreditation, but to improve our own programs. It is not our purpose to put pressure on foundations or corporations to give us financial support, but to attract their support because of the worthiness of our projects. One purpose of the council is to provide a means of sharing with one another the experiences —both good and bad—in an effort to be mutually helpful.

Alfred T. Hill, executive secretary of CASC, explained the functions of the central office with this statement:

> The purpose of the executive office in Washington is to serve the membership of the council in four areas: research, coordination, public relations, and fund raising. It is the job of the executive secretary to inform the public about the needs of the member colleges and the opportunities they offer, to encourage financial support from foundations and corporations, and to assist the

members individually and as a group in their efforts at self-improvement.

Ralph Tyler, director of the Center for the Advanced Study of Behavorial Sciences, made the following statements at the Milligan Workshop:

In examining your college's objectives, you should take into consideration these things:

1. The basic philosophy of the institution
2. The nature of the students
3. The demands made by society and the opportunities provided by society for young people today and in the future
4. The available knowledge in various fields of scholarship
5. The learning conditions within the college
6. The content of the program
7. The appropriateness and attainability so far as students are concerned
8. The balance between generality and specificity in content of academic courses

Learning is a change in behavior or the development of new ways of thinking, feeling, and acting. . . . The conditions of learning are

1. Some sort of reaction on the part of the student
2. Motivation related to satisfaction from achievement
3. A need for overcoming difficulties
4. Guidance
5. Material or "stuff" to practice on and work with
6. Repeated practice at an increasingly difficult level
7. Relation of effort to a clearly defined example or standard of excellence
8. Opportunity for measurement of progress or comparison with standards

A college should examine its program in the light of these considerations.

The college has a "moral" responsibility for providing an appropriate academic experience for whatever kind of students it admits. . . . The problem of admissions is to try to select students that fit in with the mission of the college. . . . Educational effectiveness is not necessarily greater when you admit advanced students. . . . We should remind ourselves of the danger of admitting students whom we have no basis for helping or, at the other extreme, so reduce the need for education in order to show up well on tests that we fail to admit a large group of students who represent what an institution might be able to do to bring about improved education.

If you start working on an experimental idea broad enough to modify your program, it isn't nearly so important that the idea be completely sound as that it have three other factors: (1) that it seems sufficiently promising, sensible, and important to the faculty members involved so that they are willing to dedicate themselves to the effort of trying it out; (2) that the idea that guides the experimentation is sufficiently central, that it really makes a difference, that it is not a picayune matter; (3) that there be some means of continuing appraisal, of finding out what difference it makes, of finding out whether it is working. . . . The effort to carry on an experiment, to work at a thing differently, is almost inevitably something that increases our effectiveness because of the greater attention we give to it, the greater intelligent thought we give to it, the greater interest developed by students in it.

Dr. Tyler made these comments about CASC as a group enterprise in his closing remarks at the Milligan Workshop:

CASC colleges are superior in these four respects:

1. The very fact of small size and lack of complexity of structure makes it possible to effect changes with much greater ease than is possible when there is a large structure which involves a good many problems of communication and pressures. There is a much greater potential for pioneering work in the small colleges.

2. You have a very direct contact with students and know them better than other colleges I have had a chance to work with.

3. You have adequate leadership, intelligent leadership, the kind of leadership required to move an institution ahead. Leadership, as studies have shown, is one of the very primary factors in successful achievement. Intelligent leadership, clear about what it is trying to do, clear about understanding, able to use the institution's resources wisely—this kind of leadership is here in great abundance.

4. Most important of all, you have dedication. The feeling

that you care about what you are doing provides the additional enthusiasm and energy required to do a difficult task.

In the opening general session of the Goddard Conference, President Gould of Antioch College identified four areas in which progress had been reported:

1. Reappraisal of institutional objectives
2. Participation of faculty in projects for improvement of educational programs
3. Experimentation with new courses and changes in the curriculum
4. Improvement in the quality of the student body

After identifying the four largest areas of common interest, Dr. Gould listed the four most commonly reported difficulties or obstacles in the road of progress as follows:

1. The difficulty of getting the faculty involved so that they felt a sense of responsibility for the institution's developing program
2. The general reluctance to change and the slowness with which it is brought about
3. The lack of sufficient financial resources to underwrite the desired projects
4. The poor quality of students as a retarding influence with respect to desired changes

The group was, of course, divided into subgroups for the purpose of giving close study to particular problems.

Following is a series of "quotable quotes" from the Goddard Conference. Some of them are quoted verbatim; others condense discussion or paraphrase ideas.

[Dr. Gould stated] There is always a tendency to say, "My college has the best students. We do the finest kind of work." That is not the point at all in American education today. The point is to take these students of whom there are thousands and thousands. The level is not important. We should take them where we can get them and lift them. *It is the degree of lift within the institution that is the real measurement of the progress of that institution.* We are beginning to get some of the accrediting associations to understand that. . . . It is important for this group to remember that the quality of the freshman when he comes in is not anywhere nearly so important as the quality of the senior when he leaves, and what you have done with him during that time.

The primary duty of a college president is to involve himself directly with the educational program. If leadership for an institution, in terms of its educational aims and achievements, is not going to come from the president, it is probably not going to come from anywhere else. . . . It is not enough for a president to raise money for his institution. His main job is to determine the educational directions of his institution and then do everything possible to move in those directions. If the president does things that are worthwhile educationally, he will attract to the college the kind of support that everyone is searching for.

Let's talk about the faculty. They are the most important part of your institution because it does no good to create any kind of an educational program—no matter how simple or how complex—if you don't have faculty members that are flexible enough and intelligent enough to see these things as necessary, and, therefore, to take hold of them and make them work.

One way to start building a faculty team is to ask yourself this question: "If I were the president of a brand-new college, who are the men and women in this group that I would want for the core of my institution? In other words, on the present faculty, who come the closest to being indispensable people?" Test this question by asking yourself if you would feel a tremendous loss if these people were to come to you and say they were leaving tomorrow. When you have once identified these indispensable people, then do everything possible to see that they never leave. They'll stay if they get the right kind of recognition in terms of their position in the faculty. They'll stay if you recompense them sufficiently. That doesn't mean $10,000 or $15,000 a year, but it does mean that their salaries should be brought up to a level sufficient for their needs and somewhere near to what they might reasonably expect to receive elsewhere. You may think you don't have the money, but you do. A shift of even 1 or 2 per cent from the noninstructional items to the instructional budget may be all that is necessary. At the same time when you raise salaries sharply for the important people, be sure not to give any increases to the incompetents. This is a way of serving notice without actually saying anything. In today's market there are plenty of jobs for teachers. If a man is going to be incompetent, then let him be incompetent somewhere else or, better still, leave the profession. You are doing your institution no service by clinging to those people who obviously never should have been teachers in the first place.

One way to strengthen a college is to take the key members of the faculty and put them into some kind of an informal committee to concern themselves with two matters: (1) in-service growth of the faculty and (2) improvement of the curriculum. The faculty in their efforts at institutional self-study must think in terms of the total program. Take a hint; never make any kind of dean the chairman of a faculty committee. Keep the line between the administrative side and the academic side of the institution clear cut. The chairman of a faculty committee should be a competent and respected member of the faculty. The final decisions rest with the administration.

Charles R. Langmuir, director of special projects of The Psychological Corporation, made this statement at the Goddard Conference:

> Many students in CASC colleges are superior to the average student. As a matter of fact, a third of the students in all CASC colleges are above the national norms. It is also true that about a quarter of the students in this national norms group are below the CASC average. The big thing is that there is a tremendous amount of overlap. . . . The amount of variation from college to college in the so-called national norms group is very much like the variation in the CASC group. The differences between colleges are almost as large as the differences between students within colleges.

Judson Shaplin, associate dean, Harvard Graduate School of Education, took this position at the Goddard Conference:

> First of all is the question of leadership. Where things happen there must be innovators who have conviction. Real change, real experimentation, real development does not take place in the absence of such innovators. As leaders we must be in the market for ideas. . . . In every experiment you can expect hostility,

even from people who don't know what you are doing but who in some way are engaged in the project. Even in a small experiment, the amount of hostility engendered is enormous and the only thing one can do is enter on a planned program of communication. Make sure that everybody is informed and given a chance to talk. . . . Be sure that in every project you have outside observers of some sophistication who are watching the thing go through the entire process with check points at certain intervals.

SUMMARY

This topical review of the four CASC workshops has been presented in order to indicate subjects of concern to small colleges and the level of their thinking in the areas of program development and educational experiment. These four workshops in themselves were a contribution to higher education. They constitute an example of how a group of small colleges are meeting the challenge. These meetings were important for two reasons: first, they provided an opportunity for the participants to help themselves and each other by a consideration of their mutual problems. Second, they exposed issues, raised questions, produced information, and suggested possibilities relative to small colleges on a national scale far beyond their limits of CASC membership. Some of the more important results and implications of these workshops will be considered later.

Chapter 4

CASC TESTING PROGRAM

How have CASC and its member colleges helped to meet the challenge of advancing quality education?

Their first step was to conduct an all-member student-testing program in the spring and fall of 1957. The aims of the testing program were (1) to find a basis for comparing the students in the member colleges with those in other four-year colleges of arts and sciences, (2) to stimulate the participating faculties to explore new ways of evaluating the effectiveness of their teaching methods, and (3) to secure data for planning educational experimentation.

In effect, CASC colleges were taking an inventory. They asked themselves as a group: what are we doing? How well are we doing it? Where are our strengths and weaknesses? And how can we implement the findings of test results in terms of improved teaching and new imaginative educational plans? CASC was following the advice it had already received about discovering the unique potentialities of its members and developing them as fully as possible. Never before had so large a group of such small colleges so diverse in type, function, and location, undertaken a joint enterprise in an effort to improve themselves through a cooperative effort. The results of this program are reported in this chapter for two reasons: first, because of the light they throw upon CASC colleges; second, because of their wider implications for a large circle of small colleges of which CASC is only a small segment.

In order to achieve the purposes just described, CASC received from the Fund for the Advancement of Education a grant of $56,000 to pay the costs of administering spring and fall tests, a grant of $15,000 to conduct a summer workshop to study the results and their implications, and a grant of $11,000 to conduct a mid-winter conference to follow up on the progress on plans for experiment and improvement stemming from the tests. In making these grants, Clarence H. Faust, president of the Fund for the Advancement of Education, said, "We believe the results will be valuable to the colleges individually and may well be illuminating to the present processes of accreditation of institutions." He was pointing clearly to the fact that one way to judge a product is by its performance, not by the paint on the factory. He was thus encouraging accrediting associations and financial sources to examine the performance of students in the non-regionally accredited colleges before making hasty policy decisions which might restrict the development of an important area of higher education.

TESTING PROCEDURE

The testing procedure was carried out in two stages. The area tests of the Graduate Record Examinations of the Educational Testing Service were administered to 2,450 sophomores and 1,723 seniors in fifty-two colleges in the spring of 1957. The College Qualification Test of The Psychological Corporation was given to 5,054 freshmen in sixty-two member colleges in the fall of 1957. The question is how did the scores of these students compare with those of students in other colleges?

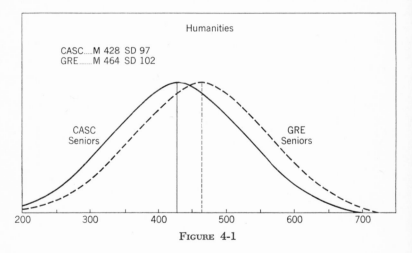

FIGURE 4-1

Since the scores for the sophomores on the Graduate Record Examinations followed the same pattern as the seniors, they will not be discussed here. The senior scores are chosen because they measure the final performance of students rather than their position midway in their college careers.

Figure 4-1 indicates that CASC seniors did not perform quite as well as those in the GRE norms group on the humanities test. However, eleven of the fifty-six CASC colleges taking this test had senior classes with average scores above the GRE average. An examination of the two curves indicates a substantial amount of overlap in the performance of the two groups.

Although the differences were not very great, students in the Eastern, West Coast, and Southwestern colleges tended to perform better than those in the Middle Western and Southern colleges. It is interesting to note that the highest faculty salaries are paid in the Eastern colleges and the lowest in the Southern.

Seniors in Catholic colleges headed the list on the humanities test, whereas those in Protestant and independent colleges tied for a close second place. The independent and Catholic colleges reported an average faculty salary of $500 greater than the average for the Protestant colleges.

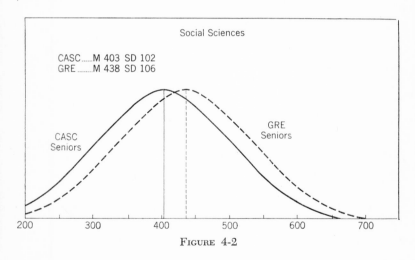

FIGURE 4-2

The results of the scores on the social sciences test showed the CASC mean to be 35 points below the GRE mean—a relatively small amount. Eleven CASC colleges ranked above the national average. In this case, as in the humanities, the Eastern colleges headed the list. However, the independent colleges topped the Catholic and Protestant colleges in that order.

The most interesting and surprising results were reported in the area of natural science, as reflected in Figure 4-3. The CASC mean was only 24 points below the GRE mean and twelve CASC colleges were above the national average. This would indicate that with relatively little additional expense in salaries and

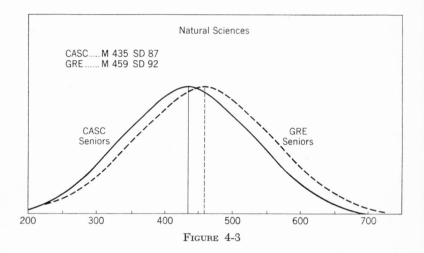

Natural Sciences

CASC.....M 435 SD 87
GRE......M 459 SD 92

CASC Seniors

GRE Seniors

200   300   400   500   600   700

FIGURE 4-3

equipment, a more selective admissions policy, and more emphasis on academic guidance these two curves might be practically squeezed together. Again, as in the cases previously reported, the students in the Eastern colleges topped the list by a slight margin. Those in the independent colleges made better scores than in either the Catholic or Protestant institutions.

BY-PRODUCTS

One of the advantages of this group testing program was that it afforded an opportunity to compare test scores against other known data in an attempt to support some reasonable conclusions or to explode some foolish notions.

Plant and Endowment

For example, some might easily believe that students attending colleges with expensive plants and large endowments would outperform those in more modest institutions.

To test this hypothesis CASC made the following analysis. The scores for all the seniors in each college were added together to make a college total score. The college total scores were then arranged in order of magnitude, and this arrangement was divided into high, middle, and low thirds. Similarly, figures for plant and endowment (assets) of the same colleges were divided into high, middle, and low thirds. A purely random distribution of the colleges based on a combination of test scores and assets would find one-third of the high-scoring colleges in the high-asset group, one-third of the middle-scoring colleges in the middle-asset group, and one-third of the low-scoring group in the low-asset group. If this were true, then the numbers in Figure 4-4 would read $33\frac{1}{3}$ per cent in each case. If all the high-scoring colleges had been in the high-asset group, and so forth, then the numbers would read 100 per cent in each case.

	L	M	H
H			33%
M		44%	
L	37%		

PcA 38%

FIGURE 4-4. Per Capita Endowment and Plant Assets Compared with GRE Composite Scores for CASC Seniors.

The analysis gave the results shown in Figure 4-4, which are not very far from purely random results. The over-all per cent of agreement (PcA), 38 per cent, is about what we would have got if we had been blindfolded and had picked the names out of a hat. Obviously 38 per cent (5 per cent above random chance) represents a small relationship between plant assets and endowment and test scores. Further evidence of this weak relationship lies in the observation that the five top-ranking test scores ranged all the way from 13 to 55 in rank order for value of plant and endowment. Conversely, the five highest in plant and endowment ranked from 22 to 45 in test scores.

In other words, as far as CASC is concerned, the conclusion is very plain. Brick and mortar do not mean high academic performance.

Operating Costs

The next question is this: "If money is spent on operations instead of brick and mortar, is there any noticeable improvement in academic performance?" The answer is yes, when the same kind of test is made.

	L	M	H
H			67%
M		41%	
L	50%		

PcA 52%

FIGURE 4-5. Per Capita Operating Costs Compared with Composite GRE Scores for CASC Seniors.

Figure 4-5 shows there is a 34 per cent better than random chance that a student in a college with high operating costs will perform better than one in a college with low operating costs. This indication is supported by the fact that the ten highest scorers on the GRE tests have an average ranking of 13 points higher in operating costs than the ten lowest scorers.

Faculty Salaries

This leads logically to the third question: "If it pays better to invest money in operations rather than in plant, then does most of this operating money go into faculty salaries? Can we conclude that better-paid teachers produce higher-scoring students?"

Figure 4-6 indicates that although the tendency lies in this direction, the relation is actually very slight. However, this tendency is somewhat reinforced by the fact that in all three area tests the seniors in the Eastern colleges headed the list and that the Eastern colleges themselves headed the list in faculty salaries. A possible explanation for the fact that the difference is not greater is that the average faculty salary in CASC colleges is very low and the range is very narrow.

	L	M	H
H			37%
M		44%	
L	40%		

PcA 40%

FIGURE 4-6. Faculty Salaries Compared with Composite GRE Scores for CASC Seniors.

Tuition

This raises another question: "Do colleges which charge high tuition turn out more successful students than those which do not?" The answer is yes.

	L	M	H
H			53%
M		37%	
L	47%		

PcA 46%

FIGURE 4-7. Tuition Compared with Composite GRE Scores for CASC Seniors.

Figure 4-7 shows there is a 20 per cent better than random

chance that students in high-priced colleges will do better on tests than those in low-priced colleges and a 14 per cent better than random chance that low tuitions and low test scores will go together. Further supporting evidence lies in the fact that the average tuition in the five highest test scorers was 300 dollars above the average in the three lowest test scorers.

Size

And now what about the notion that there is any relation between size of enrollment and academic performance? Do small colleges turn out a better grade of academic performance because of greater selectivity of students and more personal attention? Or do large colleges do better because of higher-paid faculties and more talent among the students?

The CASC answer is given in Figure 4-8 which shows a slight negative correlation between size of enrollment and performance on the GRE tests. Although the tendency is not very strong, it points favorably in the direction of the smaller college. This point is reinforced by the observation that the seniors in the smaller CASC colleges tended to do slightly better than those in the larger on all three area tests and that the average enrollment in the five highest colleges was sixty students less than the average in the five lowest. This may not be very strong support for the idea that the best things come in small packages, but it stands as a challenge until proved otherwise.

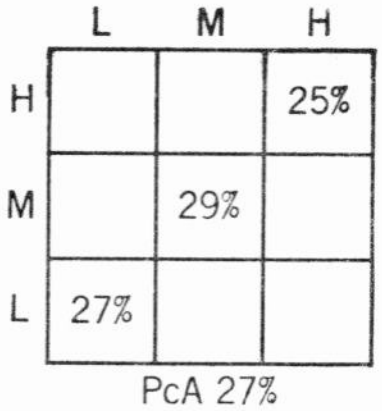

	L	M	H
H			25%
M		29%	
L	27%		

PcA 27%

FIGURE 4-8. Enrollment Compared with Composite GRE Scores of CASC Seniors.

ONE YEAR LATER

One year after the first testing program, twenty-four of the colleges repeated the GRE area tests for sophomores and seniors at their own expense. These twenty-four showed remarkable improvement in their average scores. Ten of them raised their students' performances across the board in all three areas—humanities, social studies, and natural science—whereas only two could not show any improvement at all.

In actual performance, the twenty-four colleges had an average over-all total gain of 35.4 points, of which twenty-four were achieved in the humanities, 7.5 in social studies, and 3.9 in natural science. It is notable that the CASC colleges made the greatest improvement in the area where they had been weakest on the first test, namely, the humanities.

Three of the colleges especially distinguished themselves. The King's College students raised their scores in the humanities by an average of 72 points; at Milligan College there was a 50-point improvement in social studies; and the George Fox average in natural science jumped by 57 points.

FALL TESTING PROGRAM

Having tested sophomores and seniors in the spring of 1957 to measure their performance against the norms of the Graduate Record Examinations area tests, CASC tested its freshmen in the fall of 1957 to measure its *input* compared with freshmen entering colleges in general.

To do this, CASC used the College Qualification Tests, the Cooperative Achievement Tests in Social Sciences and Natural Sciences, and the Davis Reading Test. The program was managed by The Psychological Corporation. CASC was the first group of colleges to use these tests in this way.

In reporting on the test results, Charles R. Langmuir of The Psychological Corporation noted "that the typical CASC student is somewhat below the average described by the norms." He went on to point out that between the two groups "there is a substantial amount of overlap. This overlap means that there are many students in CASC colleges whose test scores are superior when compared to test scores of freshmen in colleges in general; and, conversely, there are numerous students admitted to colleges in general who would be judged inferior by comparison with freshmen admitted to CASC colleges."

Mr. Langmuir made this further statement regarding the value of the freshman-testing program:

The important substantive results of the CASC testing program are the following:

1. Each college now has an objective description of the scholastic quality of its entering freshmen. It knows what is typical or average and how much variation among entrants is typical. It can compare its intake with the freshmen admitted to a variety of other institutions.

2. Each college is now equipped with materials *and with experience* to make practical progress in the use of tests in student personnel management (admissions, placement, guidance).

3. The council has an objective record of the level and variation of the scholastic ability and/or the secondary school preparation among and within the member institutions. The simplest statements of facts under this heading are

    a. The amount of variation within any one college is typical of colleges in general.

    b. The average level of test scores in CASC colleges is somewhat below the typical level found in the general national norms.

    c. The difference in level between freshmen enrolled in CASC colleges and freshmen admitted to colleges in general is much smaller than the difference between colleges in general and the most selective colleges of the country. This statement is an interpretative way of saying that the variation of freshman ability within institutions is so large that there is substantial overlap of the score distributions from one college to another. In simple quantitative terms, the score distributions reveal that at least 25 per cent of CASC college freshmen score above the general college average. About 60 per cent score above the twentieth percentile of college freshmen in general.

Mr. Langmuir also pointed out that the grouping of CASC colleges for administrative reasons "disregards entirely the very great diversity of their sociological locations, their financial support and control, their educational missions, and other significant factors that contribute to the large differences between institutions." He cautioned observers against the hazards of choosing any statistical measure as a standard or criterion of merit. He observed that "the data obtained in the Freshman Testing Program reflect the complex interaction of admissions policies in combination with regional variation in the quality of secondary education and the demographic characteristics of the communities."

The by-products of this testing program in such areas as geographic location, finances, and type of control have been reported as a general contribution to higher education from the experience of the CASC colleges. If the conclusions reached are valid for this group, they would probably apply with equal force to a much larger group of small colleges, of which CASC members are only a representative sample. However, two conclusions apply specifically to CASC.

The first conclusion is that the actual testing of students in the CASC colleges—although valuable in many ways—was not so important as the fact that this experience stimulated the individual member colleges and the group as a whole to ask a great many searching questions and to reexamine their assumptions, objectives, and practices. This has proved to be a healthful experience leading to the establishment of new courses, changes in the curriculum, and improvement in teaching methods.

The second conclusion is based on the surprisingly good performance of CASC students. It is that foundations, corporations, regional accrediting associations, high school guidance officers, and the general public should not be too hasty in judging an institution or a group of institutions on the basis of size of student body, plant, or faculty salaries. Since these are important elements in regional accreditation, it may be questionable to draw the line for financial support or for judgments as to the quality of education received on the criterion of regional accreditation alone. The great variety among colleges makes it inadvisable to counsel a student against attending a small college, a church-related college, a Southern college, a rural college, or almost any other kind on the basis of any one of these criteria.

The question—What is a good college?—cannot be answered hastily. The answer depends upon whether the question is related to financial support, promoting educational experimentation, encouraging the spread of Christian education, finding a low-cost college for the student with limited means, or any one of a number of other considerations.

SUMMARY

The testing program reported in this chapter is an example of one way in which the small colleges are pooling their efforts and using available resources to discover their strengths and weaknesses and adjust their programs accordingly. In effect, they measured the performance of their students against a recognized standard. But they went beyond that point. They examined the implications of these test scores with respect to the courses offered, the admissions policies, the teaching methods, and many other aspects of their total program. In this fashion they gave themselves a complete "physical examination." They were not content to observe that they were "underweight" but prescribed the diet to remedy this defect. They were not content to note that they were "nearsighted" but prescribed the "glasses." They were not content to note "poor posture" but recommended "remedial exercises" to correct this condition. In other words, they reacted to the results of their own testing program by making practical and tangible improvement wherever such changes were indicated by the scores. Some of these changes will be described in the next chapter. This undertaking in itself, as well as the mere fact of reporting it for the benefit of others, offers an example of one of the many ways in which the small colleges are meeting the challenge of *advancing quality education.*

Chapter 5

MEETING THE ACADEMIC CHALLENGE

The preceding chapter reported the results of the CASC student testing program. In effect, the colleges took an inventory in order to determine where they stood and what they should do about it.

They did do something about it. One purpose of the tests, the advice from experts, and the workshops was to get action and to produce results.

The outstanding result was that by the end of the academic year of 1958, seven members of CASC had been accredited by their regional associations, and a dozen more had had their self-studies approved by the associations. This happened because the colleges were willing and able to look themselves sternly in the eye, prescribe strong measures, and carry them out.

This chapter reports some of the things that were already being done, as well as new ideas which the member colleges decided to try as a result of fresh insights gained from their joint attack upon their common problem of improving academic programs.

It should be remembered that upon admission to CASC each member was required to fill out a questionnaire giving detailed information regarding enrollment, faculty, finances, and academic practices. Furthermore, they were asked to justify their existence in terms of competence of their faculty, service to a particular clientele, church constituency, or geographic area, contribution to educational experiment, or service to society deserving of financial support. Before the Milligan Workshop they were required to submit progress reports on their accomplishments for the academic year of 1957. At the close of the Milligan Workshop, they were required to state their plans for future improvement or experiment. At the Goddard Conference in February, 1958, they were asked to report progress since Milligan.

This chapter considers CASC colleges both as a group and as individuals in order to discuss their present practices, plans for experiment, and potentialities for the future.

THE GROUP

CASC colleges, as a group, place considerable emphasis upon improvement of instruction, professional development of the faculty, and encouragement of independence and intellectual maturity of the student. There are a number of work-study programs, remedial courses for deficient students, honors courses for advanced students, and experimental courses intended to test certain theories or capitalize upon local or regional conditions. Although all these colleges are institutions of arts and sciences, they offer a number of vocational or preprofessional courses. Because of their size as well as because of their philosophy, these colleges stress the importance of small classes, discussion method rather than lecture method, individual projects, relation to the local community, and personal contact between teacher and student.

By contrast, these colleges show little interest in programs requiring expensive scientific and engineering equipment and high-priced technical personnel. There is only a moderate amount of interest in such mechanical aids to instruction as motion pictures, radio, and television. Although CASC colleges have a large growth potential, it is fair to say that they do not intend to become large simply for the sake of size or to become weak carbon copies of the major public and private universities. They are far more concerned over serving their particular constituencies and improving the quality of their own distinctive programs. The progress reported, which was the response to the tests and workshops, can be studied in six categories.

Organic Units

Each college learned, or relearned, that it is an organic unit, greater than the sum of its parts, and not a miscellany of departments held together by a fund raiser. "Greater emphasis has been placed on integration," one college said, and thereby supplied the key word to what they were all doing—program integration. Analysis of test results had shown that the strengths in one department could be passed on to another if only by a sort of osmosis.

One, for instance, found that the simple expedient of setting up a special faculty lunch table in the college commons did the trick. Another held a yearlong faculty seminar limited to discussion of one or two books. A third had several seminars on learning theory, led by its own psychology department. In addition, this college also set up a special faculty library on pedagogy. At least two colleges sent faculty members to universities to complete their doctoral studies.

By presenting the test results to the entire student body, three colleges found an immediate increase in the use of the library; another had to increase library space by 50 per cent.

One college involved the entire corporation in an action program based on test results, advice, and findings from the workshops. The administrative officials who had participated in the CASC program went to their board of trustees with some recommendations. The board then prepared an over-all program for development of the curriculum, for capital expansion, for student recruiting, and for fund raising. The general plan was given to the faculty for implementation, and the faculty, in turn, put some students on its working committees.

Self-Study

All colleges found they had to restudy their objectives. "Why are we in business?" they asked themselves. "What are we doing to accomplish our purpose?" Questions like these were put to CASC colleges when CASC was organized and were repeated many times by CASC's friends, advisers, and the experts. Having asked themselves the questions, the colleges entered upon a wide variety of activities as a result.

Twenty members hired consultants to go over their programs, to study their organizational setup and procedures, and to make recommendations. Several others found they were trying to do too much and thereby failing to accomplish their purposes. Four of these either eliminated some courses or effected combinations of courses which better expressed their academic intentions. One cut out an entire program and entered into a cooperative arrangement with a university which gave the same program, only better. On the other hand, some found they were not doing enough. Five colleges added new courses to their curricula or increased the amount of required work in certain fields of study. One entered into a teacher-exchange arrangement with a nearby college. Another found it helpful to require each faculty member to spell out the objectives of his courses in his syllabuses.

Two colleges set about completely rewriting their catalogues. Another found itself faced with the necessity to make its faculty recruiting program explicit in terms of the college's objectives. Two, at least, discovered their presidents were overworked and hired additional administrative assistance or more faculty to relieve the presidents of the burden of routine tasks. One college found it had failed to give enough consideration to the future and therefore set up a planning committee with membership from the trustees, faculty, and alumni.

In one case there was a complete shake-up in the academic organization and program. What had been nineteen departments became five divisions, each integrated internally, and work across divisional lines was required. It was easier to deal with five divisional chairmen than nineteen department heads.

One college changed its corporate name in order better to express its function.

Analysis of Student Bodies

Every CASC college was forced to look hard at its primary constituency, its student body, who they are, where they come from, and what they want. "We had no idea," one college said, "of the wide range of abilities in our student body." The colleges found that the interchange of experiences was most helpful in trying to find out how to deal better with their students in terms of objectives and organic unity.

Eight of them expanded or intensified their counseling services. Four revised their admissions policies. Another five installed remedial programs, especially in reading and writing. Some discovered that they were not doing enough for their better students and instituted honors programs. Another tried using superior senior students as tutors for lowerclassmen. One college encouraged a wider variety of teaching techniques. Still another started a two-year terminal program because that fitted what the students wanted as well as what the local economy demanded.

Program Expansion

Nearly all the colleges which participated actively in the CASC testing and workshops were forced to concentrate on, or expand into, areas of activities outside their normal course of action or beyond their usual mode of thinking. Here are some typical examples of what happened.

One college, which presents a strong vocational and practical program, found it had to spend almost a year in philosophical discussion of what it was doing and how this was related to the church with which it was affiliated. The result was not a change in program but a clear explanation to the public of what it was doing and why; another outcome was a better organization of its program.

On the other hand, one college which hangs its entire program on a philosophical peg made a straightforward statistical study of test achievement as related to hours spent in specific courses. As a result, the college increased its requirements in science, even though it had ranked in the first five on the tests in science.

A third college which had worked up an attractive program in career and professional training found it necessary to demand more interpretative work in the classrooms and less study of facts.

A fourth college had operated a high school on its campus, and the year before the college joined CASC, the faculty had voted unanimously to continue the high school. After the college students had taken the GRE tests, the faculty voted unanimously to discontinue the high school and to concentrate on college work.

Faculty Stimulation

It was implicit in some cases and explicit in others that the test results, the workshops, and the expert advice produced strains on the various campuses. Faculties are notoriously difficult to move, and self-evident propositions do not necessarily result in obvious action. "Lethargy, faculty inertia, custom, lack of time"—these phrases reappear in the progress reports, indicating that the lively CASC administrators faced psychological blocks when they went back home and tried to get something done. In some cases drastic steps had to be taken.

Several colleges found it imperative to raise faculty salaries, which also gave them the right to demand superior service. At one college it was necessary to set deadlines for working committees in order to get the work done. Perhaps the most brutal action, to the sensitive observer, was making the entire faculty take the GRE tests, as one college did.

Confirmation of Current Practices

It must not be assumed that the workshops were wholly, or even primarily negative, purgative, and penitential in purpose or in spirit. On the contrary, beginning with the testing program, a main and overriding purpose of CASC was to find out what the colleges were doing that was better, quicker, and cheaper than what was usually done and to make these advantages known to the public and to all the member colleges. Some of these better, quicker, and cheaper programs are described in the following pages. They were, for the most part, in effect before CASC was formed and they deserve to be more widely known.

They can best be viewed by examining practices in particular colleges.

THE INDIVIDUALS

Individually, CASC colleges are characterized by originality, variety, and independence. They meet a number of specific needs. For example, one is highly experimental; another serves a small fundamentalist religious sect; a third, located in a large city, offers a long list of courses and operates a day school, night school, summer school, and extension program. One adjusts its schedule to the needs of the farm youth of northeastern Maine; another serves the Navaho Indians and the Spanish-American population of the Southwest. One has the only law school in Massachusetts outside of metropolitan Boston. One offers a course in human relations to prepare its graduates for careers in youth leadership. Several offer courses in adult education. One is the only liberal arts college in the Northeast to offer an undergraduate major in forestry. Several own and operate their own radio stations. Two have their own astronomical observatories.

In short, the variety of programs is so great that it would be impractical to report each one separately. Therefore, the following pages will discuss what appear to be the most unusual or significant developments under the following headings: improvement of instruction, unusual courses and programs, encouragement of superior students, remedial courses, cooperation with other institutions and integration with the community, and miscellaneous good policies and practices.

Improvement of Instruction

Many CASC colleges are following the usual procedures for improving instruction by helping their faculty members attain advanced graduate degrees, attend summer workshops, participate in the activities of professional associations, and engage in activities related to their professional growth during sabbatical years or leaves of absence for special purposes. However, two practices seem particularly worthy of note in this chapter: the use of faculty rating scales and the adaptation of faculty meetings to the improvement of instruction.

Rating Scales

Butler College has developed its own "Teacher Self-rating Scale." Its stated purposes are "to get your honest opinion of yourself as a teacher" and to identify various areas of strength and weakness in the college program with respect to the quality of the education. This is a relatively short and simple device for use by the administration. It is obviously intended to encourage the individual teacher to analyze his own classroom performance with a view to improvement.

Paul Quinn College uses two rating scales. "Faculty Evaluation and Classification" is obviously intended for use by the administration. It covers such matters as personal characteristics, training, experience, publications and research, membership in learned societies, general activities (on campus and in the community), teaching ability, and classification with respect to importance to the institution. This is not a self-rating scale filled out by the teacher as in the case of Butler College but rather a list of items for the administration to keep in mind in judging the faculty. It is supplemented by a second scale, the "Student Opinion Blank," covering "the total effectiveness of this course" with a breakdown of strengths and weaknesses. This is to be filled out for each course by the student and returned to the dean.

Edgewood College of the Sacred Heart uses a pair of questionnaires: one for the faculty and one for the students. The combination brings a sort of "binocular focus" to bear upon each course. For example, the instructor is asked how he stimulates initiative and thought by means of discussion, critical evaluation of reading, creative projects, and encouragement of experimentation. The student is asked to rate the degree to which he has been motivated toward research, stimulated to do wider reading, helped "to see the integration of this subject matter in other fields," and aroused intellectually. Thus the administration is provided with an evaluation of each course by both the "producer" and the "consumer."

William Jennings Bryan College uses the commercially prepared Purdue Rating Scale for Instruction, supplemented by its own "Faculty Evaluation Poll." Both are filled out by the student and cover a wide range of items including textbooks, examinations, equipment, methods of instruction, and effectiveness of the teacher. Apparently both of these questionnaires are returned to the instructors in order that they may see themselves as others see them without any reference to the administration.

John Brown University and *St. Francis College* (Brooklyn) are coupled here because both have made a rather original and imaginative use of the alumni survey as a device for improving the general college program and particularly the academic instruction. This technique offers several obvious advantages: the results reflect the opinions of people who are more mature in their judgment than they were when they were students. Opinions are likely to be more objective and impersonal because the respondents no longer have any "vested interest" in the courses or the people they are rating. A third advantage is in depth. In other words, results can be classified from graduates who have been out of college for one year, five years, fifteen years, and so on, with appropriate interpretations. Last but not least is the advantage to be gained by breadth; i.e., respondents can be classified by marital status, income bracket, type of occupation, geographic location, political leaning, and many other factors, again with appropriate interpretations.

The John Brown survey makes a direct attempt to relate academic and other experience at the college to subsequent experience in "your religious life, your vocation and employment, and your community life." The last half of the survey is particularly interesting in that it states a different objective of the university at the head of each page followed by a long list of specific academic courses and extracurricular activities. The respondent is asked to rate these items with regard to their relevance to the achievement of the objective at the top of the page. This pinpoints the answers in an unusually realistic way. Either a particular activity supports a specific objective or out it goes. At least the administration is in a position to follow that policy if it chooses.

The St. Francis survey is well worth study by any college. The results are published in a booklet under five headings: Personal Data, Occupational Data, Educational Data, the Alumni Look Back on Their College Experience, and St. Francis Alumni in Society. The college sent questionnaires to 1,779 alumni, dating back to 1893 and received a total response from 1,046 (58.8 per cent). Besides the tabulation of statistical results, the report includes a number of significant quotations which illuminate various aspects of the college program. One interesting feature of this survey is that certain sections were made parallel to the questionnaire by Ernest Havemann and Patricia S. West, the results of which were reported in *They Went to College*. This gave St. Francis a ready-made means of comparing its results against a national average. For example, Havemann and West asked alumni on a national basis whether they would have chosen the same college if they had it to do over again. St. Francis asked the same question. From the question St. Francis tried to find exactly where it stood in relation to such categories as "Ivy League," "the Big Ten," "Twenty Famous Eastern Colleges," etc. Answer: almost exactly on the national average, 78 per cent affirmative.

St. Francis scanned the college program as a whole and put the spotlight on certain courses in particular by asking its alumni to evaluate their college experiences in terms of effects upon various aspects of their adult life, such as preparation for gainful employment, marriage and family life, effective use of leisure time, and personal growth. A careful study of the accumulated responses proved helpful in improving the total effectiveness of the educational offering.

Faculty Meetings and Conferences

Many CASC colleges have used faculty meetings, conferences, and "retreats" for the purpose of improving instruction. Some examples follow.

At *John Brown University* the theme of a "faculty retreat" one year was *Improvement of Instruction*. The discussion was implemented by individual conferences between senior and junior members of the faculty. This avoided any possible embarrassment arising from the use of rating scales or from the practice of having department heads or administrative officers criticize younger teachers.

The King's College has held a series of faculty meetings designed to convey the ways in which the various academic disciplines might contribute to the improvement of classroom teaching. For example, the psychology department demonstrated how a knowledge of the principles of learning could carry over into teaching methods and the classroom situation.

At *Oakland City College* a series of faculty meetings on the general subject of improvement of instruction was divided into subheadings, such as effective use of the instructor's physical and mental energy, better use of teaching aids, professional growth, and counseling students in such a way as to develop their own powers of critical thinking.

Providence-Barrington Bible College has devoted several panel discussions in faculty meetings to such subjects as construction of examinations, grading, and motivation of students. A committee has studied syllabuses with a view to integrating liberal arts and Biblical studies, and the faculty have introduced comprehensive examinations in several departments.

Salem College has tried the novel experiment of conducting a faculty meeting as though the teachers were students, with the heads of various departments serving as instructors. The "instructor" teaches a "class" in his particular field as a means of demonstrating how the method and content of his subject support one or more of the aims of the college.

William Penn College has held faculty meetings on "improvement of instruction" under such subheadings as methods of investigating what is taking place in the classroom, selection of a good college faculty, qualities and responsibilities of administrative officers in selecting the faculty, personal and professional qualities of expert teachers, and tests of good teaching.

A survey of this list suggests that a combination of many of these items, with the addition of some professional reading and consultant service in specialized areas, might well constitute an excellent college program for improvement of instruction over a year or even several years.

Unusual Courses and Programs

Liberal Arts Reading Course

Dana College offers what is essentially a "great books" course with a new twist. Basically the plan is to select between two and four books each semester for reading and discussion by the entire faculty and student body organized into groups of twelve to fifteen students and a faculty member. One-half credit per semester may be earned in the course, or a total of four hours toward the degree.

Intensive Study Plan

The intensive study plan at *Eureka College* is carried on in the interest of efficiency: it concentrates the student's time and attention and the teacher's energies; it makes better use of space and facilities, and it simplifies scheduling. Under this plan, the academic year is divided into four terms of eight weeks each. During each term the student takes only two courses and he goes to class more often and for longer periods than he would in the usual two-semester, five-course year. There is considerable experimental evidence that by thus limiting his efforts the student can learn faster and more than he can when his time is less fully scheduled and his mind must scatter its attention.

Educational Resources Project

Advanced students at *Goddard College* serve in rural schools as part-time or substitute teachers specializing in mathematics, science, art, music, and recreation. The work is carried on in cooperation with local school superintendents. Each student's teaching program is coordinated with his program of study.

The purposes of this project are to provide more and better

teaching in rural schools, to give students responsibilities, and to find, inspire, and train potential teachers. It was begun in 1956 at Goddard and worked so well that it now includes five other colleges in Vermont and Maine (two of which are members of CASC—Marlboro and Nasson). It is financed by a grant of $112,000 from the Ford Foundation and administered by Goddard.

Comparative Cultures Program

Goddard College gives us a good example of intensive use of community resources integrated with a clear-cut academic program. In full operation, the comparative cultures program will examine three alien cultures: French-Canadian, Indian, and the French-speaking people of northern New England. It is organized so that it occupies a major part of the students' time and includes work in French, sociology, and psychology. At present, work is concentrated on the French-Canadian culture. Classroom studies are combined with visits to Canadian towns, villages, schools, and industries. Participants live with French-speaking families and attend informal seminars at the University of Sherbrooke when they are in Canada. Professors from the University of Montreal come to Goddard to lecture and discuss the practices, policies, and peculiarities of French Canada. The nonresident winter term is spent studying or working in Quebec. Each student in the program will carry on an individual research project in some aspect of French-Canadian life. This is a particularly good example of using the community resources to enrich the students' experiences, to make their learning more realistic and less bookish than usual, and to extend the subject-matter offering in this particular field beyond the normal breadth and depth of a small college faculty.

Forestry

Marlboro College is the only college in the Northeast to offer a major in forestry in a liberal arts curriculum. This means that forestry is handled as an academic discipline, like mathematics, rather than as vocational training. The course serves primarily to offer a focus for application of methods learned in other subjects such as biology, mathematics, and economics and secondarily as a means for learning a set of particular principles and methods. Specific courses in forestry are taught on a theoretical rather than practical level; e.g. the student learns how trees grow in general rather than how to grow a prize-winning white pine. At the same time, since forestry is a profession and a business, the student also works in local wood lots, for which he receives a dollar an hour instead of academic credit.

Town Meeting

Most colleges have some form of student government, but the "town meeting" at *Marlboro College* goes further than the average in the power given to it and in attendant responsibilities.

By a specific delegation of power from the trustees and by custom, the town meeting includes the entire college community: students, faculty, staff, alumni, and trustees. It functions, first, as a policy-making body: all parietal rules are made there and all decisions regarding participation in intercollegiate athletics. Through the "selectmen" (usually three students) regulations are enforced. The meeting elects a student-faculty court to sit on cases involving serious "breaches of the law." Extreme cases may be appealed beyond this court to the executive committee of the faculty.

Secondly, it serves a fiscal function. The student activity fees, which are collected by the college, are turned over *in toto* to the town meeting for administration. Thus, if the town meeting votes to field an intercollegiate team (and the college did once), all expenses for the team are paid from the town meeting treasury.

Finally, it functions as an advisory body. The "selectmen" are expected to attend the open sessions of all faculty and trustees' meetings.

The college was awarded a medal by the Freedoms Foundation in 1956 for the town meeting.

Project Courses

Marlboro College. Every student at *Marlboro College* is required to carry out at least one project before he graduates. A project may be an experiment, or it may be library research, or it may be a creative piece of work in words, paint, or music. The number of projects a student can undertake depends on his general academic standing, his performance on the comprehensive examination which is taken in the sophomore year, and on his ability and interest as demonstrated by his plan for a project. Three faculty members act as advisers and critics to each project both while it is in progress and when it is finished.

Projects at Marlboro serve two purposes. One is to put some responsibility for education where it belongs, on the student. The other is to extend the range of subject matter available to students. Projects are normally carried on in topics not offered in the curriculum, but about which the faculty committee out of its collective knowledge and experience can offer advice and judgment. This is reported as a particularly good example of one way in which a small college can stretch a dollar and stretch its faculty further. In other words, it is a partial answer to the problem of the one-man department. By using the community, the library, the faculty as a whole, and his own intellectual curiosity, the individual student may actually progress beyond the faculty talent available in a particular field.

Three-Year Plan

Students at *New England College* earn their degrees in three rather than four years through a projection of the wartime accelerated programs, even though they do not go to school the year round. Under this plan, the academic year is divided into three terms of thirteen weeks each, which makes that year seven to nine weeks longer than the usual two-semester system. To get three hours of credit, a student attends four hours of classes per week. No time is taken for final examinations; instead there are monthly hour examinations. All vacations are cut short, there is no "reading period," and no break between terms.

In addition, there is no "cut system" in effect; students are required to attend all meetings of classes and seminars. Therefore although meeting, or exceeding, the usual minimum number of hours required for the bachelor's degree, a student at New England can save one-third of the cost of getting a college education. This is a good example of the ability of the small college to experiment with the academic calendar—an undertaking which would be far more difficult, if not impossible, in large institutions with less flexibility.

Tutorial Method

The tutorial system as practiced at *Olivet College* "is based on the assumption that it is frequently more valuable for the student to spend his time reading than to be too constantly interrupted for recitations, that he should not spend so many hours in class that he has no time for study." A "tutorial" is given for one, two, three, or four students. The time, place, and frequency of meetings are determined by the tutor in relation to the subject matter and the interests of the students.

In February the freshman "who has proved himself academically" selects his "exploratory project" in a field of particular interest. This usually leads to the selection of a "trial major" in the sophomore year. This, in turn, leads to the senior curriculum.

The whole system which has been carefully evolved step by step is topped off by the honors program—"a privilege reserved for the superior student."

The entire tutorial method at Olivet is designed to put responsibility upon the student just as soon as possible, to take full advantage of individual or small-group relationships with the faculty, and to provide an automatic device for identification of talent and selection of able students through "exploratory," "trial," and "honors" programs.

Cooperative Degree Programs

To avoid unnecessary duplication of facilities and expense, several colleges enable their students to take or complete work at other colleges or universities. Within the CASC group there are three examples of how this can work.

Steubenville College has an arrangement with Detroit University whereby Steubenville students who have finished their sophomore year in required work may enter Detroit's school of engineering as juniors and go on to get their engineering degrees.

Those students at *George Fox College* who want to enter Oregon's public elementary school system take their senior year at Oregon College of Education and earn degrees from both institutions.

Northwest Christian College is wholly devoted to training future ministers, missionaries, and other church workers. Its curriculum is, therefore, limited to appropriate work in theology, music, philosophy, etc. However, it is just across the street from the University of Oregon, and Northwest Christian students may take any course they choose at the university, such as in the fields of natural science, business administration, and education. Similarly, students at the university may take courses at Northwest Christian which the university does not offer.

Humanics

Salem College is one of the four colleges where the American Humanics Foundation plan is carried on. This is a plan for training leaders in youth work—YMCA and YWCA secretaries, boy and girl scout executives, etc. The foundation was organized in 1948 by a group of Kansas City businessmen, and it finances a curriculum at the four colleges. At each college there is a resident administrator who supervises the program in general, advises the students who take part in it, and holds an endowed chair in human relations. For each college, also, there is a loan fund for deserving students who are not charged any interest. A special library is maintained at every campus. There are field trips and projects, and the students have the benefit of a guidance and placement service.

Thanks to a generous bequest to Salem College—which acknowledged the college's service to the Salem community—it was able to extend its community service to the nearby town of Clarksburg. A branch of the main campus was set up there to provide for three kinds of students: (1) entering freshmen who for various reasons, such as lack of transportation or necessity of working, cannot go to the town of Salem; (2) part-time students who have had some college work but are unable to complete it and can go to class only at night; and (3) adults who are interested only in special courses, not degrees, and who can attend only at night. It is a tribute to the effectiveness of Salem's local appeal that the Clarksburg branch opened with eighty-four students in a year of serious economic depression in West Virginia.

The Penn Program

The Penn program at *William Penn College* is a good example of a program which has been carefully thought out in terms of the college's objectives and constituency and just as carefully worked out on the operational level.

In terms of objectives, the college has kept in mind that it is a church-related school (Quaker) situated in a highly productive agricultural area. It envisages its graduates in three general groups: those who will go on to graduate school in the arts and sciences, those who will enter the professions of teaching and the ministry, and those who will return home satisfied with the bachelor's degree. For the first group, there is a sound program in liberal arts. For the second, special programs in education and theology are available. For the third group, there are programs in agriculture, industrial arts, and public service, all cast in terms of rural living. The increasing importance of state and Federal government services to rural people accounts for this.

In terms of operations, the college requires two years of general education, a two-year major in a conventional subject and a "projective experience." This latter is tailored to fit the individual for one of the three vocations (scholarship, profession, or rural living). The "experience" may be a departmental assistantship, wherein the student acts as an assistant to a department chairman by tutoring lowerclassmen, serving as a laboratory technician, or doing research. Or the "experience" may be practical —obtained off campus and at any time during the year. It is vocational, day-to-day work, such as farming, teaching swimming in a town's recreational system, or working for a veterinarian.

Students are urged to choose their vocation, and thereby their major, as early as possible in college, and then they are advised and instructed along the way as to their proper choice of courses and most fitting "projective experience."

Seminars

In the division of the humanities, social science, and art at *Hillyer College,* the seminar system is extended so that a student in the upper college (junior and senior years) can do all his work in a series of eight seminars in the liberal arts, taking four courses each year. All the work is interdisciplinary and the student carries a maximum of responsibility. He is required to undertake a research project each semester in every seminar; when he graduates, he has literally covered almost the entire range of knowledge—in science, in social problems, in history, in aesthetics, in citizenship, in philosophy, in great books, and in the art and science of communication. Only better students may do this, and they must have demonstrated their ability in the lower college. Some of the seminars are open to students not in this program who are taking regular class work in particular subjects.

Honors Work

Honors work begins early at *Gordon College,* in the sophomore year if the faculty judges a student capable of it. Each research project or honors program is individually tailored; it may require attendance in regularly scheduled classes or it may not. A student is admitted to this program by petition, and if he wants to continue in it, he must renew his petition each year. The level of achievement demanded by the college is almost at the straight-A level. On the other hand, when the work *is* straight A the student is rewarded by extra points toward graduation. Thus an A is worth four points to a student in the honors program but only three to a student who is not. For the student who spends three years in this program, there is some required work: attendance at the honors seminars which deal with the history of the West, especially the history of ideas. In the sophomore year, the period covered extends to A.D. 700, in the junior year from 700 to 1700, and in the senior year from 1700 to the present.

Encouragement of Superior Students

Goddard College has developed a plan to increase the self-reliance of the student by decreasing the frequency of class meetings from three times a week for the first-year student, to twice a week in the second year, to once a week in the third and fourth years. In fact, the last semester of the senior year is almost entirely devoted to independent study. This would seem to be especially appropriate for the mature and superior student.

One requirement for graduation at Goddard is the successful completion of a major independent study. Such studies occupy all or most of a student's time during his last semester. They are intended to be integrative and are conducted under the supervision of one faculty member, with others called upon for consultation when necessary.

Gordon College has conducted for several years an honors program open to sophomores, juniors, and seniors "with virtually an A average in their previous experience in college." Students are allowed relatively free range in the selection of courses, are permitted to investigate special topics, and are not bound by the usual standards of attendance. This is practically a tutorial system. Students in this program must meet normal A standards in order to receive a B grade.

George Fox College has been experimenting with an "intensified studies program" designed to put a premium on the ability and maturity of the superior student. A superior student is identified at the end of the first semester of his freshman year by a careful screening process. His major professor then helps the student select a faculty committee to help him plan, execute, and evaluate his chosen program for the next 3½ years. The program consists of wider and deeper reading than would normally be required—particularly in fields related to the student's main project. More than usual use is made of source materials. There is greater than average leeway in such matters as class attendance and examinations. Tremendous incentive is provided, awarding the superior student a scholarship for full board, room, and tuition, with the understanding that he must return this to the college before receiving any academic credit if he drops out before the completion of the course. As the student advances, his program becomes more and more individualized and tutorial in character.

Remedial Courses

Butler College gave its students a test taken from a paperback edition of *Thirty Days to a More Powerful Vocabulary* by Funk and Lewis. After an evaluation of the scores, students were assigned exercises of thirty minutes a day for thirty days. All teachers were to allot the first ten minutes of each period to this vocabulary experiment. This proved to be a very inexpensive approach to an increasingly common problem.

Milton College conducts what it calls a "student rehabilitation program." For a number of years, about thirty students in the first semester and fifteen in the second have been transferring to Milton after an unsatisfactory academic experience in larger institutions. After an examination and study of their past performance, Milton has admitted these students on probation and has put them back on their feet academically. As a safety valve, the college has set up rather strict probationary procedures so that a student who does not measure up to the required performance within a specified time is automatically dropped. The result has been that about 75 per cent of the group have been restored to good standing and about half of this number have chosen to stay at Milton rather than return to their first college. Provided it were carefully guarded, so that it would not become an academic scrapyard, this service of academic rehabilitation might well be generally offered by hundreds of small colleges able to salvage students who never quite "find themselves" on a large campus.

The King's College has been conducting an experiment in delayed classification. For example, a student can remain a freshman for two years without dropping out of college. Thus, at the beginning of college, the poorer student has a longer chance to get on his feet. There is a strong social incentive for the weak student to catch up with his class and to earn the privileges of advancement which are otherwise denied to him.

Western New England College has an agreement with four high schools whereby a student can make up a year's work by taking a six-weeks summer course at the college. The teachers come partly from the college faculty and partly from the schools. The college thus kills several birds with one stone: it uses its plant in the summer, cooperates with the schools in its community, and meets the needs of poorer students.

Cooperation with Other Institutions and Integration with the Community

Brooklyn Historical Institute. The Brooklyn Historical Institute of *St. Francis College* (Brooklyn) affords a particularly good example of how a city college can utilize opportunities in its local community. The institute is composed of a group of seniors working under the joint direction of a faculty committee and the county clerk. The scheme has two purposes: (1) to awaken in the student an awareness of the rich historical background of the local community and an understanding of its economic and social development, and (2) to awaken in the local community an awareness of the contributions of the college to local life. What actually happens is that the students conduct their research in historical and other areas from first-hand sources, in a realistic situation, under an authority actually engaged in current local government. The outcome of this investigation is a written report on which faculty and students collaborate.

The Haskins Laboratories Project. The Haskins Laboratories, in New York City, was founded in 1935 for the express purpose of scientific and educational investigations for advancing the frontiers of knowledge. It is an educational institution for basic research and training in certain pioneer areas which involve several scientific disciplines. It is interested in conceptual rather than occupational goals.

Ever since its founding a hundred years ago, St. Francis has included science in its curriculum. In answer to the current national shortage of scientists and mathematicians, St. Francis is determined to do its part by providing a steady stream of undergraduate students prepared to go on to graduate and professional studies and to help fill the demand for trained research experts and scientists.

From these two statements it is obvious that St. Francis and Haskins Laboratories should get together, and they did—to their mutual advantage. The college and the laboratories made an agreement under which qualified students are permitted to engage in microbiological research at the laboratories under supervision of the Haskins staff. In return, Haskins staff members hold formal appointments as associate professors and research advisers at the college. For the college, this arrangement has meant a strengthening of its science offering far beyond the normal limits of its department. This is an excellent example of interinstitutional cooperation.

The College of Steubenville cooperates with two nearby hospitals. One hospital sends its student nurses to the college for their basic science courses. The college sends its faculty members to the second hospital to teach courses in psychology, ethics, and sociology to student nurses.

Steubenville has turned the phrase "town and gown" into a slogan for cordial college and community relations through its courses for adults. Classes are offered in the evenings and on Saturdays for those who wish to learn while they are still holding down full-time jobs. The classes range from hobby courses to full degree programs. As an "extra dividend" the college runs a "community institute"—an annual series of lectures by members of its faculty open free of charge to the public.

Fort Wayne Bible College has a five-year nursing program.

The girls take their first year at the college, their next three years at the Lutheran Hospital, and their fifth year back at the college. They are then graduated with a B.S. degree in nursing, are fully registered nurses, and can practice anywhere.

Western New England College has capitalized on its location in Springfield, Massachusetts, the heart of New England's industrial area. It has an enrollment of 250 students in a course in air force reserve management, under contract with the local United States Air Force Reserve Center. As a part of the Air Force program for promoting its officers, this is basically a course in the development of executive techniques for officer personnel. The course runs for 24 two-hour sessions during the year and is offered in Pittsfield and Greenfield in addition to Springfield.

Upland College has adjusted its program to the needs of its community by offering adult courses in the areas of management and leadership improvement. These courses are for the benefit of industry and community and degree credit may be earned.

Miscellaneous Good Policies and Practices

Eastern Mennonite College has the distinction among small colleges to have an observatory equipped with a Spitz planetarium, a motorized orrery, a 4-inch Zeiss refractor, a 12-inch reflector, a 6-inch equatorial refractor, a 20-power 5-inch Japanese binocular, and a 25-power 4-inch German binocular. It has attached a classroom-laboratory suitable for astronomy classes and guest groups. Eastern Mennonite was selected as an official "moonwatch station" and its team of twenty-two student moonwatchers sighted and reported data on the first two Russian Sputniks.

Eastern Mennonite College also has a 10-watt educational broadcasting station (WEMC) operated and staffed by students under the supervision of a licensed faculty director. This provides students with experience in engineering, programing, script writing, and a great variety of performances, with a total daily average of three hours. Plans are under way to offer credit courses and adult education to the community over the air.

Gordon College is experimenting with the use of seniors to assist in teaching survey courses in their major fields to underclassmen. These selected seniors conduct discussion sessions, act as tutors, and in general personalize the instruction of a large survey section. It is believed that this experiment will result in a better grasp of their fields for the seniors and may develop a desire on their part to make college teaching a career. The professor sits in on various discusion sessions in order to retain control over the survey course as well as to evaluate the performance of his seniors.

Ricker College is located on the northeastern border of Maine, where many of the students need to work on the farms on Saturdays. Therefore, Ricker has been experimenting with its weekly class schedule with interesting results. Instead of scheduling a class for three 50-minute periods in traditional fashion, the college has arranged for certain classes to meet for one 100-minute period followed a couple of days later by a 50-minute period. This eliminates Saturday classes without reducing the total amount of class time. It also preserves an interval of two or three days between meetings which would be impossible if three classes were to be scheduled in a five-day week. The advantage of the double period followed by a single has proved particularly effective in languages, literature, history, and economics. In such subjects as these, longer periods for discussion proved desirable. In conjunction with this scheme, Ricker is emphasizing the conference or discussion method of teaching, with a substantial amount of independent reading, and it is minimizing the traditional lecture method.

St. Mary of the Plains College has been operating a 12-week summer session, divided into four 3-week periods, designed expressly for liberal arts and professional training of elementary school teachers in service. The 1957 enrollment in the four summer periods averaged about ninety, most of whom lived on campus. This is a clear answer to the critics of higher education who complain that so many college plants lie idle three months of the year.

Western New England College has recently been given equipment amounting to the equivalent of $50,000 by the Standard Electric Time Company. The "McIlroy Fluid Network Analyzer," as the equipment is called, analyzes pressure of water flowing through a city pipe system; it can also be used for gases and other kinds of fluids. Only three other colleges in the country have this. This machine is of tremendous importance in training students in the analysis of hydraulics and measurement of fluid pressure.

SMALL COLLEGES OF THE FUTURE

The preceding pages of this chapter provide a review of what the small colleges of CASC are doing collectively and individually. The observations reported have implications far beyond the CASC membership. In the light of these observations I shall yield to temptation and make a few predictions regarding the small colleges of the future.

Administration

On the subject of trustees, A. V. Wilker of Union Carbide told the council last August at Nasson:

> . . . too often the selection of a trustee is based upon the theoretical value of his influence, coupled with a desire on the part of the college to build political fences with respect to the particular denomination to which the college might be related. The value of a board of trustees does not depend upon its size or upon the number of distinguished and honored men making up the board, but upon those with sufficient dedication to put their shoulders to the wheel and really do the kind of job their assignment calls for. A dozen or so working members with a sense of responsibility mean more to me than several times that number of men of reputation and position and title who, complacently, accept the trusteeship of the college as an honor and grace the annual meeting every year or so with their dignified presence. Therefore, if I had any interest in the financial support of a particular college, the first thing I would want to know would be whether the college has a reasonably capable president for its administrative head, and whether it has an adequate board of

trustees of men of dedication coupled with a willingness to work, and whether the president and the board worked well together.

When you consider the controls of bureaucracy manifested in state and Federal government and the red tape of big business today, the trend toward conformity is so impressive that you wonder if there is any place left for "rugged individualism." Where can a man with imagination and a will of his own turn for a satisfactory outlet for his talents? One place to look is in the small colleges. There are challenging opportunities for trustees and presidents in these institutions which are not hindered by tradition but are free to experiment boldly with both the content and form of the academic program. The field is wide open for administrators to demonstrate their originality, imagination, and courage in discovering new educational techniques, serving neglected areas of our society, and pioneering on frontiers where those who have already "arrived" have no reason to venture.

According to W. H. Turner, executive director of the United States Steel Foundation:[1]

> Thoughtful persons have pointed out that the nonconformist often is the essential grit which gives traction to our cultural, social, and economic life. Teachers, artists, scientists, men and women in small and large organizations—in government, business and industry, the church, in unions, or in other affiliations—best serve their own individuality and work for progress when they are responsible to ethics and intellectual integrity, as contrasted with kowtowing to paychecks, royalties, transitory popular preferences, or to what may be momentarily fashionable but of questionable taste. A dying society is one in which there is no room for faith of and in the individual, no orbit for conflict, no space for the nonconformists.

In April, 1957, U.S. Steel gave $10,000 to the Council for the Advancement of Small Colleges. It repeated this grant in the spring of 1958. In addition, U.S. Steel has made two grants of $25,000 each to members of CASC and a number of grants of

---

[1] William H. Turner, "Education for Responsibility," commencement address, Pacific University, May 26, 1957.

$1,000 each. This would seem to afford an example of backing up the above policy in a way that counts.

Faculty

Teachers have always been 75 per cent missionaries, and I hope they always will be. However, if able young men and women of the future are to be attracted into, and retained by, this profession, small colleges must do better in their competition against large universities, industry, and government. I believe they will.

I predict that teaching in the small college of the future will present one of the most attractive careers on the American scene. This is one of the last stands of individualism, one of the few spots where a man can call his soul his own and need not submerge all his achievements into the anonymity of the group. I believe there will be a shift in the attitude that has been referred to as "the careful, cautious, security-ridden generation now in our colleges." I saw this happen once before. In 1948 I was studying the postwar Emergency Training Scheme for Teachers in England. I discovered upon a personal visit to twenty-five of the fifty new teachers' colleges which had sprouted up all over England that those entering the teaching profession were doing so from a mature sense of vocational calling. As one man expressed it: "Before the war I was an accountant in a large firm earning twice what I will make in teaching, but now I am tired of dealing with figures and things. I want to spend the rest of my life dealing with people and ideas." That's it. The small college will be one of the best places left in our over-adjusted, overorganized society where a man can deal with people and ideas.

In the future, there will be less distinction between the so-called teacher and the so-called scholar. We tend to think of the teacher as a low-paid civil servant concerned primarily with methodology and very little with content. We regard what we call the scholar as an individual living in an ivory tower very much concerned about the passive periphrastic but not much interested in communicating with his fellow man. I believe that the two extremes will tend to approach the mean so that the teacher-scholar of the future will be a more cultured person than the teacher of today and a warmer and more dynamic person than the scholar of today. This will be particularly true in the small college, where there is less specialization and more general education, less research and more teaching, than in the large university.

In the future, it may be well to remember the words of former President Sills of Bowdoin College: "Excellent teaching in wooden halls is better than wooden teaching in marble halls."

Programs and Procedures

Let's take something simple, the academic calendar: nine months of study, three months of vacation. There is nothing sacred about it. Just because it has always been that way it doesn't always have to continue that way. I predict that many colleges—and particularly small ones—will operate twelve months a year. I predict they will operate on the quarter system instead of the semester system. Possibly the terms will be staggered so that one-fourth of the students are always on vacation while the other three-quarters are keeping their noses to the grindstone.

I predict more Saturday classes and more night classes. Again, the present pattern of five classes meeting three times a week is not a law decreed from on high. It is a custom, a convenience that has developed to meet a need. If the need changes, the custom will change with it. This may happen in the small colleges sooner than in the larger ones, because they are more flexible. They are freer to take a chance. They have less academic machinery to unwind and disassemble and then gear up all over again.

There will be more accelerated programs whereby an able student can achieve a bachelor's degree in three years.

There will be a marked increase in the number of small so-called community colleges. I do not refer to two-year junior colleges which have more or less appropriated the term "community college" and informally "copyrighted" it as their own. I refer to small colleges of all types, two-year, four-year, liberal arts, and specialized. In other words, I anticipate a general broadening of the base of higher education particularly in the freshman and sophomore years by the dissemination of scores of small colleges close to the people, close to local industry, close to the typical American small town.

Another very marked trend in higher education will become more pronounced in the future, i.e., the development of the two-year, or junior, college. There are already more than six hundred of these institutions in this country with more than three-quarters of a million students. The direction is toward the development of more public junior colleges and fewer private.

Frequently one of two things happens. (1) A student attends a junior college for two years, takes a so-called terminal course, usually vocational, and calls it a day; or (2) at the end of two years, he transfers his credits and continues his last two years of college but usually in a large state university. The net result is that the traditional, four-year liberal arts college is bypassed completely or, to put it another way, is caught in a squeeze between the two-year public college on the lower level and the four-year public college on the upper level.

I predict that (1) if the small private liberal arts colleges are complacent, old-fashioned, narrow-minded, conventional, and high-priced, they will surely die; (2) if they are vigorous, bold, imaginative, competitive, varied in their programs, and low in their costs, then they will grow in size, increase in number, and extend their importance and influence in American higher education. Today the small colleges stand at the crossroads of their destiny. Which way will they go?

I predict admission to college at an earlier age—again particularly in the small college where the young student has less difficulty in finding himself than in the larger institution.

Because of the teacher shortage, if for no other reason, the small college of the future will not spoon-feed its students as it has in the past. I believe it will force intellectual independence and responsibility on them at an earlier age. I predict that students of the future will do much more independent learning through reading and research of their own.

The small liberal arts colleges will carry an increasing load of teacher preparation of the future, and with more methods courses in the liberal arts colleges and more subject-matter courses in the teachers colleges, the day will come when you can hardly tell them apart.

There will be more regional and national cooperation and sharing of facilities and personnel among the small colleges. For example, a dozen colleges belonging to CASC are all located in New England. Suppose these twelve colleges were to pool their resources in order to engage the services of a distinguished lecturer in history or science or religion. Now suppose they sent him to each campus to give a special seminar for two weeks. In this way they would each individually remain small institutions but they would be large in the sense of commanding the services of a high-priced top-quality professor which no one of them alone could afford.

Let us reverse this idea and apply it on a national scale. Suppose a college in Maine were to send ten of its top students for the first semester of their junior year to Oregon and the second semester to Texas. At the same time colleges in Oregon and Texas would be engaging in a similar exchange. The students in this case would have the advantage of being in a small college all through their college careers. Yet, they would have attended three colleges instead of one and they would have seen three areas of the country instead of one. If the whole is greater than the sum of its parts, the cumulative effect of this experience would be much more than to triple the value of their higher education. I predict this will happen in the small colleges.

I make still another prediction for the small colleges. They must plan their admissions policies and academic programs in order to meet different demands from those met by the large colleges. I am not suggesting for one moment a lowering of standards. However, I do suggest that the small colleges may be able to perform a service to society by giving special prep-school or remedial noncredit courses to hundreds of students who have come from high schools where their college preparation has been inadequate. I am not referring to the boy or girl of low mental ability. I am referring to the average or even very bright boy or girl who has come from a small rural high school with inadequate staff and facilities and from the large city high school with mass-production methods and a heavy concentration of commercial courses. I believe that the small colleges of the future will have an increasingly important role in counteracting the mediocrity of public school mass production.

Oliver C. Carmichael, former president of the University of Alabama, has said,[2] "the most encouraging fact in the college and university world today is the unprecedented ferment and concern for the improvement of their programs which is discernible in every section of the country and in every type of institution. In practically every college . . . discontent with the program is the characteristic of these postwar years."

This discontent is particularly strong in the small colleges of CASC. These are small colleges with big ideas. They will increase their enrollments; they will improve their faculty salaries; they will invent new courses and discover new teaching methods.

Because of the problem of too many students and not enough teachers, the large universities are already experimenting with all kinds of mechanical aids to teaching: movies, closed-circuit TV, tape recordings, etc. This trend will continue. On the other hand, it will automatically encourage the growth of many small colleges where the contact of the individual professor with the individual student will be prized even more highly as the secret of successful education.

Most significant of all, the small liberal arts colleges of twenty-five years from now will be increasingly important as outposts on the frontiers of higher education. I agree with Wade Arnold of Affiliated Public Relations, Inc., when he said at the Nasson

[2] Oliver C. Carmichael, "Major Strengths and Weaknesses in American Education," *Proceedings of the Eighth Annual National Conference on Higher Education,* National Education Association, Washington, D.C., 1953, p. 12.

workshop: "In this jungle of pressures to make us all dress, look, think, and act alike, the small college is a ray of light, a reminder that teachers in communion with students are more important than buildings." He would keep it experimental, keep it fresh, keep it as untraditional as possible. It would be sure and sudden death for the small college to try to imitate the bigger one and thereby become a weak carbon copy. For their very survival, the small colleges depend upon their competitive spirit, their determination to do something and to do it faster, and cheaper, and better than their rivals. As one writer on this subject has said, "the history of heresy is the history of progress." So it will be in the future—particularly for the small colleges. Only those which are unique, which are truly "better mousetraps" in Emerson's phrase, will survive.

It is by the practices listed in this chapter and by the changes predicted above that small colleges will meet the academic challenge of the future.

Chapter 6

NATIONAL VISIBILITY

"What you need to do is to increase your national visibility," said Wilson Compton. Then he went to work and helped CASC do just that—increase its national visibility.

First—before retiring as the president of the Council for Financial Aid to Education—he published and distributed widely a pamphlet entitled *The Small Non-accredited College: Its Place in American Higher Education*. Then he accepted the national chairmanship of the CASC board of advisers and in that capacity served as spokesman for the small colleges at one national meeting in Miami and six college-and-industry luncheons in Los Angeles, San Francisco, Portland, Boston, Pittsburgh, and Cleveland. On these occasions he held press conferences, talked on radio, and appeared in television interviews. In addition to this, he permitted CASC to print and distribute one speech and one article, and he attended numerous regional meetings, directors' meetings, and workshops. He gave a commencement address at Salem College and served as financial adviser to the board of trustees of Upland College. This was voluntary service on his part. It put real meaning into his statement quoted in the dedication of this book that he was "a friend of the small college and proud of it."

HOW CASC MEETS THE CHALLENGE

In the meantime CASC itself had not been idle. In the spring of 1957 it printed and distributed its first major mailing piece, *Small Colleges: An Untapped Resource.* This was a sort of directory or handbook intended for corporation and foundation executives. The first nine pages told the group story with respect to the needs of the members, sources of income, faculty salaries, potentialities for expansion of enrollment, and issues related to accreditation. This was followed by a 2-page spread of statistics. The booklet concluded with a paragraph on each of the members. This was the first presentation ever made of the facts and figures about a substantial group of non-regionally accredited colleges. It attracted approval and support.

The second major publication was *A Directory of Small Colleges* printed for CASC by McGraw-Hill Book Company, Inc. This pamphlet first saw the light of day at the CASC 1958 national meeting in January at Miami Beach. In less than a year over 15,000 were distributed to libraries, schools, churches, educational associations, the press, and by request to about 5,000 persons. A revised and up-to-date version of this directory is included in the Appendix of this book. It is obviously intended to give parents, prospective students, school officials, and the general public information about enrollment opportunities available in this group of small colleges.

Within less than three years, CASC had various aspects of its story told in the *Bulletin* of the Association of American Colleges; the American Alumni Council *News* and also its *Educational Fund-raising Guide; Pride,* the bulletin of the American College Public Relations Association; *Higher Education,* the publication of the U.S. Office of Education; the *Educational Record* of the American Council on Education; *College and University Business; School and Society; The New York Times;* the *New York Herald Tribune;* the *Christian Science Monitor; Time; Changing Times; Better Homes and Gardens,* and several other publications.

Station WNEW in New York ran a series of spot features on CASC colleges as a public service; a number of other radio and television stations covered various CASC workshops and meetings. One of the most important ways in which CASC has told its story is through the publication of its regular monthly newsletter, supplemented by special mailing pieces to cover particular subjects.

In June, 1958, *Better Homes and Gardens* published "These Colleges Want More Students." The article listed eighty-eight colleges, of which forty-six were members of CASC, all of which had room for more students than had applied for admission in the coming September. The following October, *Life* carried an article by Henry W. Wriston, "How Colleges Can Handle the Throngs," which pointed out that many good colleges still were underpopulated in spite of the greatly increased national enrollment. Wriston said: "American institutions of higher education, as a whole, had 12 per cent fewer students than they could handle. This figure admittedly is accounted for to a large degree by non-accredited institutions."

Now, Wriston was a little too sweeping in his generalization; his remarks did not apply to the CASC colleges. They had been on a vigorous recruiting campaign, and they contributed more than their share in filling the 12 per cent shortage of students. In the fall of 1958 CASC enrollment was 14 per cent larger than the previous year, a rate of increase more than double that of all American colleges.

Figure 6-1 illustrates the growth in the CASC colleges and symbolizes the way they have increased their visibility to the college-aged population. Full-time enrollment of the members in 1956, when CASC was founded, was 18,915. Their estimated enrollment for 1970 was 37,865. The curves A, B, and C show three ways by which the 1970 estimate could be reached. The most optimistic curve—the one marked C—predicted an enrollment in September, 1958, of 22,865 students. The actual figure was 22,883, or better than the optimists had hoped. On the basis of these data it is now expected that the hoped-for 1970 goal will be reached by 1965.

One factor which contributed to this growth, other than the vigor of the colleges, was the distribution of 15,000 copies of *A Directory of Small Colleges* to prospective students, their parents, and to college guidance officers in secondary schools. The names of the students and parents who requested—or bought— the *Directory* were sent to each member college, thereby giving it a greatly expanded "market."

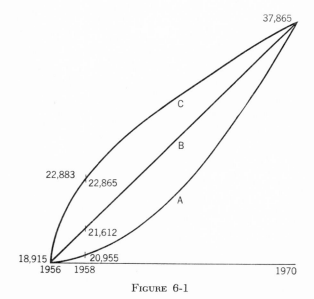

FIGURE 6-1

IMPORTANT NAMES

Another way in which CASC attracted favorable attention to its members and enhanced their prestige in the eyes of the public was by inviting outstanding men to serve as speakers on national programs, to act as directors of workshops, and to serve as consultants both to the group as a whole and to individual members.

CASC has made a successful effort to focus the attention of the foundations and corporations upon the potentialities of its members, to serve the public by spreading the story of additional room for students, and to capitalize upon the potentialities of the group to give national recognition to individual colleges which had never before had more than local reputations. This has been an effort at sound public relations—not publicity or advertising in the usual commercial sense.

PANORAMA OF THE COLLEGES

Once more—as in other cases already mentioned in this book —the impact of the group is impressive. CASC colleges are following the recognized standard procedures with respect to catalogues, brochures, mailing pieces, newspaper coverage, consultant services, and professional staff. Under the influence of their organization, most of these colleges now belong to the American Alumni Council and the American College Public Relations Association. These contacts have proved extremely stimulating, informative, and beneficial to them.

It is obvious in surveying the public relations programs of these colleges that lack of money has limited the range and quality of their efforts. For example, although CASC colleges publish many excellent catalogues, better type, better layout, better design, and better content could be achieved in this area. TV, radio, movies, and the press might be used more extensively. CASC faculty and administrators could contribute much more than they do now to professional journals and commercial magazines. Much more could be done to send able speakers from their faculties, administrations, and student bodies into their communities. They could do much more to attract national figures to their campuses on special occasions. It would seem possible for these colleges as a group to capitalize on the combined resources of all their alumni to help solve their financial problem. The time has clearly come for CASC colleges to assume a position of leadership and serve as spokesmen for all small colleges on issues of national importance.

CASES

As in dealing with other problems, the CASC colleges individually have shown much imagination and originality in telling their stories to the public. Following is a partial list of the membership—a selection of those colleges with particular practices which recommend themselves for possible adaptation by other colleges.

Detroit Institute of Technology

Divisional Organization. DIT has found that the alumni of its separate schools respond better in terms of an appeal to their own specialized interests than to an appeal from the college as a whole. Therefore, it has set up separate alumni associations for the school of engineering, the school of business, and the school of arts and sciences. The officers of the original alumni association serve as a central alumni council composed of elected representatives from the three alumni groups.

School and Campus Visits. DIT has encouraged its professors to visit the high schools and participate in their "career day" programs. It has also invited high school administrators to visit DIT for informal luncheon meetings to become acquainted with the college.

Publicity. DIT has used direct mail, posters, car cards, newspaper advertisements, and television programs in addition to conventional releases throughout the immediate Detroit area.

Faculty Participation. DIT has encouraged a vigorous program of participation in educational and professional meetings in its area, and it has established a fine relationship with other executives in institutions of collegiate rank with major industries.

Eastern Mennonite College

Publicity. EMC has published *Looking at Our Educational Future,* a leaflet on its future enrollment prospects which is a good statistical study and at the same time a sound mailing piece for fund-raising and general public relations purposes.

George Fox College

Herbert Hoover. Former President Hoover attended George Fox before going to Stanford. It was through the efforts of President Milo Ross of George Fox that CASC secured the letter of endorsement from Herbert Hoover which has been printed in the handbook, *Small Colleges: An Untapped Resource,* and widely circulated through the newsletter. The name of Herbert Hoover as a distinguished alumnus is of great importance to George Fox.

Publications. George Fox publishes a journal and a bulletin for and by the faculty. Both of these receive wide distribution.

Alumni Solicitation. The alumni list had not been corrected for twenty years. As a result a class-by-class personal registration drive was undertaken recently, with the alumni association raising $8,000. This was unprecedented and most gratifying. The work is continuing. New alumni chapters have been organized in seven cities.

Alumni Participation. George Fox reports that in its recent drive, a few classes rated 100 per cent and a great many averaged 80 to 90 per cent. If this figure were compared to the American Alumni Council standards, it would certainly break the national record.

Alumni Trustees. George Fox has recently doubled the number of its alumni trustees from three to six. The association has started publishing a new alumni news.

Alumni Program. The alumni have been sponsoring dinners in honor of their graduating high school seniors. These dinners have been held in ten different places and are apparently very successful in recruiting students.

Goddard College

Faculty Publication. During a recent year, articles written by members of the faculty appeared in seven professional journals. In addition to this there has been a greatly increased news coverage by the Vermont newspapers.

Seminars. Goddard makes an annual practice of holding seminars on important subjects. An example of this was its conference on "The Role of Liberal Education in Developing Leadership for Expanding Economy." This conference was held in New York City, with representatives from business, labor, and education. The college has also made a special point of attracting a variety of groups to its campus during the winter when its students are taking a nonresident term away from the classroom. Such groups customarily hold conferences of several days' duration. This is an excellent way to call the program of the host institution to the attention of influential people all over the country.

Gordon College

The college uses a considerable amount of local and national state advertising aimed at recruitment and fund raising. It sends out monthly publications to a mailing list of seven thousand, operates a speakers' bureau and sends out faculty and students, and reports news releases of close to two hundred clips from New England newspapers each month.

The alumni secretary maintains a well-equipped office for placement and counseling, sends a periodic magazine to his association mailing list of 2,500 people, promotes a $30,000 annual fund, and leads regional chapters of the association in many on- and off-campus activities climaxed by June alumni day.

Hillyer College (University of Hartford)

Industrial Advisory Committee. Hillyer has an industrial advisory committee of seventy-five men representing major industries in Hartford. They meet periodically at dinner to discuss their needs and how the college can help to meet them. The college has one employee who gives all his time to calling on industry in an effort to find ways to serve. He never asks for money but rather what the college can do to help solve industrial problems. This college is very closely integrated with the community life of Hartford in every respect.

John Brown University

Alumni Relations. The college has conducted a program of stimulation for the alumni to hold group meetings, form local chapters, participate in fund raising, engage in student recruitment, and contribute to projects for improving the physical plant.

Miscellaneous Publicity. The college has carried on a program of *advertising* in national magazines. It has distributed a monthly magazine to an extensive mailing list. It has presented the "John Brown Hour," a continuous program of spot broadcast announcements regarding the college. It has sent its choir and other musical groups on trips and thus carried information about the school along with their musical programs. It has sent its tumbling team to give demonstrations at high schools, and it has participated in *college day* activities in the larger high schools in its area. It is in constant touch with the newspapers.

Marlboro College

Summer School. The college rents its facilities in the summer to the Marlboro Music School from which the college gets not only money but nationwide publicity.

Newspaper Coverage. In the spring of 1957 Marlboro had almost a full-page spread in two consecutive Sunday editions of the Providence *Journal-Bulletin*—complete with pictures and a full story of campus life. This was a description of and news about a college with an unusual program—not paid advertising.

Milligan College

Summer Workshop. The summer workshop of 1957 (like the one held at Nasson in 1956) resulted in excellent public relations for Milligan. One hundred and twenty people from sixty colleges from all parts of the country were on the Milligan campus for a full week studying the results of the CASC student-testing program. This was of national significance and the name of Milligan was featured in many articles on this subject.

Milton College

Slogan. Slogans have to be treated with some care; however, Milton has one which seems successful, "Large enough to serve you, small enough to know you."

Report of Contributions. Milton has made a pie chart of its contributions from July 1, 1955, to June 30, 1956. This includes 689 donors who gave $73,488.61. The percentages were as follows: $41\frac{1}{2}$ per cent from business and individuals outside Rock County; 25 per cent from businesses and individuals in Rock County; $12\frac{1}{2}$ per cent from 1,240 alumni; $8\frac{1}{2}$ per cent from businesses and individuals in Milton and Milton Junction; 11 per cent from the Wisconsin Foundation of Independent Colleges, and $1\frac{1}{2}$ per cent from two individuals.

Alumni Trustees. Nine of the twenty-seven trustees are elected by the alumni.

Community Services. The college offers cultural opportunities to the community in semimonthly public convocations, courses in religion and art open to auditors, an annual art display, concerts, athletic contests, lighted tennis courts, a library for community use, special services at Christmas and other times, clinics for choral conductors, and work with the boy scouts.

Alumni Questionnaire. Milton has conducted a survey of 405 former students which produced helpful suggestions on the size, character, equipment, and student services offered by the college.

National College

Honorary Trustees. National College has established a board of honorary trustees, enrolling a large number of men to help in financing and assisting the college throughout the immediate Kansas City area.

Providence-Barrington Bible College

Alumni Support. More than 30 per cent of the college's 1,300 alumni give regularly, but the amount is small because nearly half of them are pastors and missionaries with small incomes.

Radio and TV. Providence-Barrington has produced an educational TV series which reaches 78,000 homes in southeastern New England.

Miscellaneous. The college reorganized its mailing list into twelve separate divisions and it is cultivating each one distinctively. Special emphasis was given to (1) a three-month alumni fund drive which has increased the percentage of participation as well as the amount, (2) parents' association drive, (3) a direct-mail campaign to 250 industrial and business leaders.

St. Francis College (Brooklyn)

Alumni Loyalty Fund. St. Francis has had an alumni loyalty fund organized for about five years. During the last year it netted a little over $7,000. It is estimated that the effectiveness of solicitation was about 40 per cent and the average contribution about $14.

Public Relations Director. St. Francis operates a public relations office with a full-time director and sends out a steady stream of mimeographed news releases. The college reports more extensive newspaper coverage and an increase in advertising. It has contacted employers with promotional literature and increased its publicity to educational magazines. It also has organized a student group which has proved effective.

College of St. Joseph on the Rio Grande

On its CASC questionnaire of September, 1956, St. Joseph reported as follows:

We certainly could use a public relations and promotional person also, but have been unable to do so because of lack of funds. As a result, faculty members have to dabble in this type of work, if it is to be done, with the result of damage to their regular work and failure to accomplish results from promotional activity. . . . We have no wealthy people among our alumni, most of them are teachers. They help as their small means will permit.

In the progress report of May 15, 1957, St. Joseph has this to say,

The committee on public relations kept the college events in newspapers; members of the college staff visited high schools within a radius of 50 miles to speak to seniors; instructors and professors gave talks at state meetings, PTA meetings, etc. There has been a decided increase in alumni interest in college affairs. The alumni association has given a benefit dinner, tea, and dance; it is presently sponsoring a musical comedy to be given on four successive nights in July for the benefit of the building fund. The letter men sponsored a bazaar in November. The College Guild held a benefit card party. All of these were a more than fair success.

St. Meinrad Seminary

The majority of the alumni are ordained priests and, therefore, have a very low income. The small-town community is not in position to give much financial assistance. St. Meinrad has joined the American Alumni Council, and it has also increased its mailing list to alumni by 200 per cent by including nongraduates. The college has established a publicity office and gets out a quarterly newsletter. Not all its alumni are priests, and the seminary has recently organized a lay alumni association with local chapters in nearby cities.

The College of Steubenville

Tenth Anniversary Convocation. During the year, the College of Steubenville scheduled several new events including a tenth anniversary convocation at which four industrial neighbors celebrating anniversaries received commemorative citations. It is always flattering and a good policy to invite people to your birthday party—especially if it happens to be their birthday too.

Tabor College

Radio Program. The alumni sponsor a "College Chapel Hour" which is broadcast as a special project. This radio voice of the Christian college is now being aired by thirteen stations in the United States, one station in Canada, and one in Ecuador.

Miscellaneous. The college publishes brochures, bulletins, and student and alumni newspapers. It keeps in touch with the local newspaper and home-town newspapers. It sends two choir ensembles to visit various churches. The faculty serve in church and service organizations.

CONCLUSION

Any sound public relations program should be regarded as a service to the public, not a trick or a pressure campaign. This has been the main objective of the CASC program—to inform corporations and foundations about their opportunities to develop the untapped resources of the country to meet a national crisis. It has also attempted to serve the community at large by making known the availability of room for more students at low cost.

So far as the individual colleges are concerned, one may well observe that they have tried to "win friends and influence people" through a variety of methods. However, the predominant idea has not been "What can you do for the college?" but "What can the college do for you?" The emphasis among these small colleges has been upon cultivating their own alumni, their own trustees, their own church constituencies, and their own communities. These efforts are gradually resulting in increased prestige and greater national visibility. "The Noise You Hear Is Progress!"

Chapter 7

OPERATION BOOTSTRAP

CASC has been tagged "Operation Bootstrap"—an enterprise in self-help, a project to strengthen its members by pooling their resources. This label is particularly appropriate to a group of colleges in which it is not uncommon for the president to don overalls and swing a hammer or wield a paintbrush, in which many buildings have been erected with the help of students working side by side with union labor, in which business managers have characteristically shown great ingenuity in stretching a dollar as far as possible. Some of these stories will be told in detail at the end of this chapter, but first it is important to view this group of colleges as a whole.

COMPOSITE PICTURE

Until CASC was organized there was no reliable body of financial or statistical information about the non-regionally accredited colleges as a group. The first assignment of the CASC office was to assemble this information for the benefit of its members and also as a service to corporation and foundation executives who had some sensible and penetrating questions to ask before making any contributions in support of these institutions. For example, how inexpensively can a college operate and still stay in existence, let alone do a good job? Is the business management or "housekeeping" in these colleges really up to date and efficient, or is there a great deal of inefficiency and waste?

The most reliable and recent figures for this group as a whole are those reported in response to a CASC questionnaire distributed in the fall of 1956 for the fiscal year just completed. At that time, the fifty-two charter members of CASC had a total investment in endowment and plant assets of $60,901,292 or about 1.2 million dollars each. Since their total enrollment was 25,115 students, their capital investment was about $2,420 per student, compared with $5,467 per student reported two years earlier for liberal arts colleges across the country.

The fifty-two original members reported a total operating cost of $14,248,544 or an average of $274,000. This meant that a typical college was spending about $560 per student—extremely low.

According to the National Education Association,[1] the median salary paid to full-time instructional personnel in 343 private colleges in 1956 was $4,448. The comparable figure for CASC colleges was about $3,681. In the spring of 1958 when Seymour Harris reported in *The Atlantic*[2] that the typical president's salary was $11,500, the typical CASC president's salary was hardly more than half this amount.

These figures go a long way to support the statement made by the McGraw-Hill Publishing Company[3] that the damage to the nation from "the underpayment of our college and university faculty members over the past fourteen years . . . has minimized the devoted service of many faculty members who have loyally stuck to their jobs . . . [they have been] subsidizing these institutions by their financial sacrifice. This is a menace to the cultural and intellectual life of the nation . . . [and] to our national security."

From the standpoint of the student, CASC colleges are a real bargain. In the fall of 1956, in three-fourths of the charter mem-

[1] *Salaries Paid and Salary Practices in Universities, Colleges, and Junior Colleges, 1955–56,* National Education Association Research Bulletin 34, Washington, D.C., October, 1956, pp. 111–163.

[2] Seymour E. Harris, "Who Gets Paid What," *The Atlantic Monthly,* May, 1958, pp. 35–38.

[3] *Business Aid to Our Colleges and Universities,* McGraw-Hill Publishing Company, Inc., New York, 1954. Reprint of five editorials from McGraw-Hill publications.

bers, tuition and other fees ranged between $300 and $600, with a median of $400. By comparison, the median tuition charged in forty-six state universities for out-of-state students was $412. According to a study made by the U.S. Office of Education (HEW) in the summer of 1957, the total expenditure per year for full-time undergraduate students attending public colleges was about $1,500.[4] Since the median in CASC colleges at this time was $850 for all college charges including room and board, this would leave a balance of $650 for the CASC student to spend on clothes, books, travel, and recreation before reaching the level of the boy or girl in the state university. The comparable cost to the student in the typical private college was estimated at $2,000, leaving the CASC student with a leeway of $1,150 dollars for "extras."

When the question is asked, "How do the small colleges meet the challenge financially?" an honest and straightforward answer is that they pay low salaries to dedicated teachers and administrators. They operate in simple utilitarian plants rather than in luxurious buildings; they offer programs which can be handled without elaborate and expensive scientific and engineering equipment, and they serve a serious-minded group of students who do not demand some of the fashionable luxuries associated with large stadiums and fraternity life. The result is a sound, simple, low-cost education for those who want it.

This writer is concerned with two main points: (1) to call to the attention of professional educators and the public in general the fact that this large group of low-cost, little-known institutions are already operating at a time when their services are in great demand and (2) to call to the attention of corporations, foundations, and individual philanthropists the importance of strengthening both the capital and operating funds of these colleges so that they not only can keep going but can do a much better job.

[4] Ernest V. Hollis, *Costs of Attending College*, U.S. Office of Education, Washington, D.C., 1957.

MANAGEMENT SURVEY

Ever since CASC was started, one of its main ambitions was to have a management survey of all its institutions in order to find out whether the "housekeeping" was good or bad and which corners needed dusting. This survey was the basis of the third summer workshop held in August, 1958, on the campus of Michigan State University. The unique feature was the bringing together of the three top administrators, the president, dean, and business manager, in order to coordinate the academic and non-academic operations of the member colleges.

The management half of the workshop was under the direction of Irwin K. French, executive director of the National Federation Consulting Service. Mr. French was the chairman of the research committee for the well-known *Sixty College Study* sponsored by the Fund for the Advancement of Education in 1953–1954. In order to gather financial and statistical information, Mr. French sent out questionnaires to all the CASC colleges in the spring of 1958. He reported his findings under the headings of common problems, budget planning and control, purchasing and auxiliary enterprises, and efficiency and economy through shared resources.

Two big stories emerged from this survey. The first was an answer to the question: how do CASC colleges compare with other small colleges—particularly those in the *Sixty College Study?* The second was an answer to the question: are the current practices in the CASC colleges good or bad and where do they need improvement? The answers to these questions are given below.

Comparison with Sixty College Study

Table 7-1 compares a sampling of seventeen CASC colleges which submitted their figures in a way which permitted comparison and a group of twenty colleges with enrollments between two hundred and six hundred taken from the *Sixty College Study*.

TABLE 7-1. COMPARISON OF COSTS IN GENERAL AND EDUCATIONAL
EXPENDITURES (in per cent)

Median	17 CASC colleges	20 colleges
General and administrative	25.2	29.1
Instruction	50.5	48.4
Library	4.5	4.9
Maintenance and operation of plant	19.2	15.6

Two of the CASC colleges had received regional accreditation, and several others had completed most of the preliminary steps toward accreditation. All twenty colleges selected from the *Sixty College Study* were accredited. A comparison of median expenditures on a percentage basis is shown in Table 7-1.

This table leads to the conclusion stressed so many times in this book: the similarities between CASC colleges and other colleges are much more striking than the differences, particularly at the middle of the range.

These figures suggest a question: if these CASC colleges are so similar to the others, why aren't they regionally accredited? The CASC colleges are actually spending slightly less proportionally on administration and more on instruction. They are spending almost the identical percentage of their budgets on the libraries. But "inadequate libraries" has always been one of the greatest obstacles to accreditation. A difference of 4/10 of 1 per cent could hardly be described as "seriously inadequate." The fact that the CASC colleges appear to be spending slightly more proportionately for the maintenance and operation of their plants could be interpreted as an attempt to clear up a hidden deficit in deferred maintenance or it might mean a healthy growth pattern; either would be good practice.

In short, the answer to the first question is very plain. If a corporation or foundation wants to know how CASC colleges compare with similar institutions in the *Sixty College Study* before making an investment in them, the reply is that a cross section of CASC colleges (not every one individually) compares very favorably.

Composite Picture of Good Management

Table 7-2 lists good management practices, with the percentage of CASC colleges adhering to them.

TABLE 7-2. GOOD MANAGEMENT PRACTICES

Practice	Per cent of colleges
Good organizational and line-of-communication chart	62.5
Accepted accounting methods and financial reporting	70.0
College operates on a budget	80.0
Dormitory equipment furnished by college	90.0
Students do own "housekeeping"	77.0
Dormitories are monitored	67.5
College operates bookstore	90.0

One should not conclude that because a particular institution does not follow all these practices it is therefore poorly managed. This list is presented as an indication of the trends. A college which was very far out of line presumably could justify its deviation for special reasons.

In making observations and drawing conclusions about the operation of CASC colleges, Mr. French made these points which are summarized and paraphrased as follows:

Trustees. There is no need for concern over the wide range in the number of people serving on boards. The important point is the amount of interest the board takes in the institution. Boards which meet only once or twice a year—unless they have very active committees—are not giving enough attention to their institutions. Quarterly meetings are more desirable.

President. One of the principal criticisms of the president in a small college is that he tries to wear too many hats at the same time. It is not the president's job to function as dean, business manager, dormitory supervisor, superintendent of buildings and grounds, and director of public relations all at the same time and still represent the college to the public, report to the board of trustees, raise money, and direct academic policies. None the less, there is a tendency in this direction in the small colleges which are so underdepartmentalized that the president attempts to carry too many specialized responsibilities.

Budgets. Although CASC colleges generally follow a good standard procedure in the preparation of budgets, there is an indication of inadequate follow-up and control. The trouble with most budgets is that they do not reflect the institution's submerged or hidden deficits in the form of low salaries, obsolete equipment, and deferred maintenance. Two budgets should be prepared: one to show what *can be done;* the other to show what *ought to be done.*

Purchasing. A composite picture of good purchasing practices in small colleges shows the following characteristics: a full-time purchasing agent is not justified; the chief business officer can handle the purchasing function. Requisitions and purchase orders should be required from all departments; there should be no direct buying by department heads. Office supplies should be issued from a central storeroom. Invoices should be approved by the chief business officer and paid before the tenth of the month. Economies should be effected by standardizing many types of requirements and by ordering in bulk for long periods in advance.

The answer to the second question, "are the current practices in the CASC colleges good or bad and where do they need improvement?" is also plain. As a group, the CASC colleges are following good management practices. Furthermore, they are alert to their opportunities for improvement. Several have conducted full-scale management surveys. There is always room for improvement in efficiency, but it is reasonable to say that the majority of CASC colleges are aware of the importance of "good housekeeping" and are alert to their opportunities in the area of nonacademic operations. Sharing experience and being brought face to face with the experts at the Michigan Workshop has stimulated many CASC colleges; a number of them are now engaged in streamlining and modernizing their management policies and practices. Many of their business managers have attended the institute for college business officers at Omaha University. Many of them have arranged their financial reporting to conform with the procedures recommended in the *Sixty College Study* by the American Council on Education or by their regional associations. Many are members of the National Association of Educational Buyers. Several have availed themselves of Federal building loans.

SOME CASC MANAGEMENT PRACTICES

Spending Money to Earn Money. Many CASC colleges believe they are too small and too short of operating funds to be able to afford a full-time administrative staff. Some, however, have learned that a few dollars invested in the right people pay off.

George Fox College, with an enrollment of fewer than 150 students, hired an alumni secretary and a public relations officer. In less than three years this college (1) increased alumni giving from $21,000 to $35,000 annually, (2) reduced its debt from $144,000 to less than $16,000, and (3) built a student union which is a model for small colleges.

At *Gordon College* a similar increase in alumni contributions was brought about when the college engaged an alumni secretary. But this college added a novel, and logical, function to the office. The alumni secretary acts as a placement officer and job counselor; he thereby puts the college to work for the alumni while they are still undergraduates and serves the very practical purpose of launching its graduates into the business and professional worlds.

The North Central Association of Colleges and Secondary Schools states that when it evaluates a college it looks for "evidence of growth." It found this evidence at *Morris Harvey College,* accredited by North Central in 1958, when it looked at the development program. Morris Harvey is run by a director who has these aides: assistant development officer, alumni secretary, director of public information, and director of community services. Like many CASC colleges, Morris Harvey is a "community college" in the sense that its aim is to serve the needs of its immediate area, Charleston, West Virginia. A director of community services is a necessary officer, especially if the college's TV classroom is to be a success, which it is at Morris Harvey.

Operating in the Black. A few CASC colleges actually take in more money from student fees and endowment income than they spend; i.e., they can show an operating profit without a cent of income from gifts. All of these are community colleges like Morris Harvey, except that they enroll only commuting students and do not operate dormitories and dining facilities.

The most notable example is *Hillyer College* of the University of Hartford where, as they say, "our seats never cool off." They run three sessions daily—a day school from 8:15 A.M. to 4:15 P.M., a twilight school (chiefly for local public school teachers who are seeking advanced degrees or higher certification) from 4:30 to 6:15 P.M., and a night school (which has the largest enrollment) from 6:30 to 9:15 P.M. All this is done with the barest minimum of administrative personnel and the maximum, in CASC, of faculty salaries.

The other CASC colleges which are in the black are *Detroit Institute of Technology, St. Francis College* (Brooklyn), and *Western New England College.* Like Hillyer, they have their largest enrollment at night, which more than halves the investment per student. Two of them, Detroit and Western New England, further cut capital costs by renting space from the local YMCA. Western New England applies what it teaches in engineering, commerce, and law, by paying its faculty on a per diem basis rather than on a semester or yearly basis as is customary. In each of them the educational emphasis is practical—commerce, engineering, and education—aimed at supplying its community with the skills it demands.

Utilization of Space and Time. Not all CASC colleges can run two or three shifts a day, especially the rural colleges. Some of these colleges have found other ways to put their facilities to profitable use.

Goddard College has a long winter work period starting before Christmas and ending about March 1. During this time the students are off campus working on jobs or on independent research. The college, however, is busier and more populated than at any other time during the academic year. It is open for conferences, workshops, and meetings, which are local, state, or national in scope. (At one of them, for instance, Gordon Clapp, then head of TVA, told a group of Vermont businessmen why a TVA would not work in Vermont, which they were surprised and, in spite of their traditional Republicanism, disappointed to hear.) These conferences are either self-supporting or are financed by foundation grants, and the college earns a profit on its auxiliary enterprises during a time of year when it is most expensive to house and feed students.

Twenty-eight CASC colleges run summer schools. Probably the most successful in many ways is the one at *St. Joseph's on the Rio Grande.* This session has, in effect, two aims: one philosophical and one a practical application of its philosophy. In the Southwest there are sometimes strong feelings, not always of affection, between English-speaking and Spanish-speaking people, and a kind of mutual segregation is practiced. St. Joseph's does not believe in any kind of segregation as policy and one of its chief "products" is teachers. The problem is to teach enough English to the sons of the conquistadors to enable them to get through college and to be able to teach English in the village schools. Much of this work is done in the summer school, and remedial English is now a specialty of the college.

Support from Nonacademic Operations. There are still other ways in which CASC colleges can effect more efficient and economical use of their facilities. A rural college near a large university can neither operate as a community college nor run a summer school, but competition from educational giants does not dismay the imaginative administrator.

Madison College, for instance, turns to its philosophy of work and study and to its own resources to run itself on a self-supporting basis. All students work a minimum of eighteen hours per week on the college farm, or in the food-processing plant, or in the milk plant. They are paid for this work and the brighter and more energetic student can earn more than what the college charges in fees, for the number of hours of permitted work in excess of eighteen depends on the student's grades. Thus it is possible to graduate *summa cum laude* and get a sizable check along with a diploma. The college also runs a 220-bed hospital in which premedical and medical technology students can get experience. Finally, when the college wants a new building, the student body provides a labor pool accustomed to work and having the necessary skills.

At *Roberts Wesleyan College,* they made shrewd use of a grant from the Gannett Foundation. They built a factory and leased it to a plastics molding firm. The rent for the factory provides income to the college, and its operations provide jobs for students who have to work their way through college.

Marlboro College rents its entire facilities to the Marlboro Music School during the summer. This enterprise employs the college business staff and earns the college a large increment in free publicity through the twice-weekly concerts featuring such artists as Rudolf Serkin, Martial Singher, and Alexander Schneider. (Van Cliburn was a student there for a couple of years.)

A large part of Marlboro's 350-acre campus is worn-out Vermont pasture land. This land is ideally suited to Christmas trees, and 20,000 are now planted there, paid for by a commercial tree grower who rents the land from the college. This college also has developed a steady business in the sale of maple syrup made from its own trees by its students and faculty.

Unusual Budgetary and Accounting Procedures. The heart, soul, and muscles of sound management lie in budget making and control. No better example of how to do this can be found than at *Northwest Christian College.*

Its budgets, in expenditures, for the forthcoming year always equal the income for the present year, which, in turn, always includes a reserve for bad luck. Since this college always manages to increase its yearly income from gifts (chiefly from bequests and the church), it is always in the enviable position of being able to increase faculty salaries, or to add books to the library, and to expand its program.

St. Mary of the Plains has a main building, valued at 3.2 million dollars, on which it pays no interest, principal, nor rent. It was built by the religious order which founded the college and is carried on the books of the order, partly as a matter of conscience and partly to help the college balance its budget more easily.

At *Rio Grande College,* they were troubled by one of the most notoriously inefficient units of all colleges, the library. By using statistical and graphic methods, they were able quickly to sort out the books by category of use-frequency and thereby greatly to increase efficiency without extra cost.

Rio Grande also faced up to the problem of scholarships versus mounting costs, by increasing the student loan fund. This was a bold step for a small college struggling to enroll more students. They were to find, of course, that they had anticipated the National Defense Education Act of 1958 which eliminated undergraduate scholarships entirely from the Federal program and provided only for loans.

Goddard College is the most experimental of the CASC colleges and does nearly everything with a difference. However, it did adopt the sixty-college accounting system for the curious reason that it expressed, in the business office, a more exact description of its educational aims and methods than did the system it had more or less invented for itself.

Probably *Nasson College* offers the best possible case study of how to run a small college. Although a detailed report cannot be made here, a few of its accomplishments can be mentioned and a few reasons for them given.

In seven years' time the capital assets were increased sixfold, from $300,000 to $1,800,000. The college was changed from "an institute for females" to a coeducational college, and its enrollment rose from 60 to 320. An excellent and profitable research and testing program in antibiotics is being carried on. When John C. Hazeltine, Commissioner of the Community Facilities

Program of the Housing and Home Finance Agency, inspected Nasson as a possible recipient of a loan he noted that it was a college "where every dollar will do the work of two" and approved the loan.

All this was achieved by the right combination of analysis and action. First, the situation was examined. The original institute was set for "useful education" of women. This idea was kept, since there was no vocation-centered college in Maine. The trustees were persuaded to make the college universally useful by admitting men. (This necessarily involved changing the attitudes of the trustees.) Then "useful" had to be usefully defined. Among other things this turned out to include home economics, which at Nasson has a wider meaning than household management. Graduates from this program have gone on to manage the dining facilities at such colleges as Radcliffe, for instance.

Progress also meant setting reasonable goals. For example, it was planned to reach an enrollment of three hundred by 1960, but this figure was passed in 1958.

Finally, it means, as good management frequently does, being hardboiled. No program, no matter how well conceived and planned, is better than the people who will carry it out, and they, in turn, must be intellectually and morally loyal to it. It is noteworthy that none of the faculty at Nasson in 1951, when the development program was begun, are now on the staff. It is also noteworthy that during this period of growth, the college increased its plant from seven buildings to fifteen and raised its faculty salaries 50 per cent per capita.

Milligan College and *St. Francis College* (Maine) afford two unusually good examples of the use of the installment plan of paying for a college education.

The director of admissions at Milligan used good judgment and imagination in at least two cases of considerable "human interest." The first concerned a young woman whose father owned a turkey farm and operated "the only feed mill in town." He was reported to be a substantial citizen with excellent credit. The difficulty was that his business was seasonal and he did not have the ready cash available to send his daughter to college in the middle of September. Mr. Stahl of Milligan reports a conversation that went about as follows:

STAHL: When will you have the cash?

FATHER: Not until Thanksgiving or Christmas when my turkeys are sold.

STAHL: Well, here's one bird who will wait until you sell your birds to collect for the year's tuition.

FATHER: Well, I never heard the likes of this; but if you mean what you say, I'll send my daughter to your school.

Result: the daughter attended Milligan for two years, taking a secretarial course, and secured a fine job in the regional office of a national corporation.

The second case had to do with a young man who was the valedictorian of his high school class and had won a regional oratorical contest. He had made an enviable reputation in the field of agriculture and was interested in biological sciences. He had no money.

About six o'clock [says Mr. Stahl] the father returned home, and I discussed my plan with him. Briefly, it was this. At that time our tuition, fees, room, and board, at Milligan College was only $690. We offered a valedictorian scholarship in the amount of $125. We then provided work in the amount of $150. This left a balance of $415. I said to the father I would let him pay that $415 over a twelve-month period at the rate of approximately $35 a month. The father said he only made $6 a day. "I am a day laborer on the public roads. That $35 represents six days of hard labor, or a week's wages; but I am so anxious for my boy to get a college education that I would be willing to pay a week's wages every month in order for my boy to go to school."

The boy returned home from a job at a service station which he had secured just a week or so prior to this, and we explained the plan to him. He was rather reluctant at first, but with family insistence agreed upon this arrangement. At 8:45 P.M. that same evening, we were packed, with his clothes for one semester in my car; and we were on our way to Milligan College.

The boy completed four years' work. Each year during the four years he led his class and was graduated *summa cum laude*.

At the end of his senior year, he was granted a $1,200 fellowship at the University of Tennessee to major in biological sciences. The second year this scholarship was renewed in a similar amount, and he is now at the University of Tennessee for a third year with a $1,200 grant.

Father Thibodeau of St. Francis College reports as follows on a plan which is not general but has worked successfully in several cases:

We accept a good student. He pays whatever he can while attending St. Francis College and promises to pay the balance monthly after graduation. As of now, there are seven students under this plan. Depending upon the individual case, some were granted up to five years to pay a year's board and tuition. Here is a typical example: student A could not have attended college last year had it not been for this plan. He is now a junior at St. Francis College and is paying for his junior year. He will start paying for his sophomore year after graduation at the rate of $12 per month. An interview with this boy revealed that we should offer him the same privilege for his senior year. This means that student A might need up to ten years to pay his board and tuition for his sophomore and senior years. By the way, we are very willing to grant this boy such a privilege not only because he is a good student, but also because he is very grateful.

The president of Milton College has tried a novel idea called "tuition plus." When the first semester grades go out just before Thanksgiving, the president writes a personal note to the father of each student. In the body of his letter he states very bluntly that it is the responsibility of the trustees to secure in addition to the regular amount for tuition another item of at least $100 in order to balance the operating budget. The president then invites the parents to participate by making a tax-deductible contribution. This has brought very good results.

CONCLUSION

It should be clear from this chapter that small struggling colleges have to live by their wits in order to exist. They have to pinch pennies and stretch dollars. They have to develop local resources, and most of all, they must have courage and imagination. In other words, they are in the true American tradition of "Operation Bootstrap." This is how they meet the challenge of increasing operating costs and a depreciated dollar.

Chapter 8

MEETING THE FINANCIAL CHALLENGE

The urgency of adequate financial support for higher education is so great that it seems important to consider the relation of the small colleges to the national scene in this matter. In short, how do the small colleges meet the financial challenge? Let us arrive at the answer to this general question by a consideration of four subquestions:

1. How do the small colleges regard Federal aid?
2. What has been the recent history of private support for small colleges?
3. How does CASC as an organization help its members financially?
4. How have the small colleges shown initiative and originality in raising money for themselves?

WHAT ABOUT FEDERAL AID?

CASC made a careful poll of opinion from its membership on the question of Federal aid. Although the replies to the questionnaires on this subject indicated strong views on both sides of this issue, the weight of majority opinion was in opposition to assistance from the Federal government.

Those who opposed Federal aid did so for many reasons. Some were against it on religious grounds. They felt that Federal aid would violate the principle of separation of church and state.

Others interpreted "aid" to be synonymous with "control" or, worse still, "interference." One president pointed out that if Federal aid were added to the support already being received from taxes by the state colleges, the combination would be so great as to put the private colleges completely out of competition. Strong opposition was expressed to the expense and inefficiency which always accompany the bureaucracy of any project run by the Federal government.

Several presidents expressed their views affirmatively rather than negatively. One man, for example, said, "Rather than running to the tax trough, let's take pride in doing the job the American way; let's create a situation in which students and parents take pride in bearing their fair share of the load, rather than feeling inferior or slighted unless a scholarship is available."

Those in favor of Federal aid tended to minimize the threat of control. "The old bogie of government control of the colleges is by this time fairly well laid away," said one president. The most impressive argument in favor of Federal aid was that the job ahead of us in the immediate future was so overwhelmingly great as to be well beyond the possibilities of private financing. This would leave no other choice but Federal aid.

Three forms of Federal aid received support: (1) loans and scholarships for students; (2) long-range loans for construction of buildings of all types; and (3) tax deductions for gifts, for tuition, and for membership in the educational profession.

In the spring of 1958 the National Education Association made a study[1] indicating that in 1956 Americans spent 43.4 billion dollars, on liquor and cigarettes, automobiles, and recreation. During this same year, according to figures from the U.S. Office of Education, we spent 1.7 billion dollars for both capital and operating expenses on private higher education. In other words, for every dollar we spent on private colleges, we spent more than $25 on less important items.

Whether they choose to do so or not, the implication of these figures is that Americans could certainly keep the control of

[1] *Compare the Costs,* National Education Association, Washington, D.C., 1958.

higher education in private hands for the price of a few drinks and smokes, a few rides, and a few movies. They certainly are not without alternatives to Federal aid.

WHAT ABOUT PRIVATE SUPPORT?

This point of view is strengthened by the joint report of the American Alumni Council, the American College Public Relations Association, and the Council for Financial Aid to Education in the spring of 1958.[2] According to this report, 910 institutions in 1956–1957 received $832,937,123. This was a 62 per cent increase over their receipts for 1954–1955. Frank H. Sparks, president of the Council for Financial Aid to Education, predicted that this amount would easily double within the next five years. The figures reported here represent voluntary contributions from foundations, corporations, alumni, and individual philanthropists.

In the spring of 1959 the Council for Financial Aid to Education estimated that corporations were contributing to education at a rate of less than $\frac{1}{4}$ of 1 per cent of their income before taxes. The law allows corporations to contribute up to 5 per cent. Again there is still adequate room for the expansion of private support of private education.

In the spring of 1959, the American Alumni Council reported that less than 25 per cent of the alumni solicited were actually contributing to their college alumni funds and that an average gift was only $32. Once more there is plenty of room for the expansion of private support for private higher education.

Comparison of CASC Colleges with the National Averages

Table 8-1 presents a comparison between the 65 members of CASC, 327 coeducational colleges, and the 904 colleges and universities discussed in *Voluntary Support of America's Colleges and Universities.*

These figures show that the coeducational colleges are receiving

[2] *Going Up: Voluntary Support of America's Colleges and Universities, 1956–57,* Council for Financial Aid to Education, New York, 1958.

TABLE 8-1. SUPPORT TO CASC COLLEGES COMPARED TO NATIONAL
AVERAGES AND TOTALS

Group	Per college	Per student	Total
CASC	$ 94,131	$228	$ 6,119,524
Coed	574,111	667	187,734,150
All	904,168	510	817,378,017

six times as much money on a per college basis as CASC colleges, nearly three times as much on a per student basis, and
thirty times the total. The CASC picture is even more discour-
aging when compared with "all" colleges; these are receiving
nearly ten times as much on a per college basis, over twice as
much on a per student basis, and over one hundred and thirty-
five times the total.

A comparison of the percentage of distribution of support is
presented in Figure 8-1. Since 90 per cent of the CASC colleges
are church-related, it is not surprising that their church constituencies account for nearly one-third of their gift support in
comparison with much lower proportions in the national averages.
It is noteworthy that CASC colleges on a percentage basis are
substantially ahead of the national averages on support from
individuals and from bequests. They are close enough to the
national picture in all other categories not to warrant special comment except when it comes to foundations. From foundations,
coeducational colleges are deriving nearly eight times as much on
a percentage basis, and "all" colleges are benefiting nearly ten
times as much as CASC colleges.

Obviously the big money from the large foundations is going
to the large colleges and universities. This confirms what former
President Hoover said to K. Duane Hurley in his letter of May 2,
1957: "I have long been convinced that the failure of our great
foundations to develop and support adequately the some fifty-odd
small non-accredited colleges is the greatest gap in their otherwise great contribution to American education."

From this graph one may conclude that the small colleges of

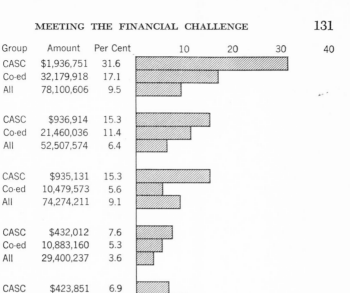

Source	Group	Amount	Per Cent	10	20	30	40
	CASC	$1,936,751	31.6				
Churches:	Co-ed	32,179,918	17.1				
	All	78,100,606	9.5				
	CASC	$936,914	15.3				
Individ:	Co-ed	21,460,036	11.4				
	All	52,507,574	6.4				
	CASC	$935,131	15.3				
Bequests:	Co-ed	10,479,573	5.6				
	All	74,274,211	9.1				
	CASC	$432,012	7.6				
Trustees:	Co-ed	10,883,160	5.3				
	All	29,400,237	3.6				
	CASC	$423,851	6.9				
Corps:	Co-ed	19,163,153	10.2				
	All	76,897,762	9.4				
	CASC	$411,825	6.7				
Alumni:	Co-ed	12,132,394	6.5				
	All	62,654,683	7.7				
	CASC	$247,794	4.0				
Foundns:	Co-ed	59,637,540	31.8				
	All	319,085,152	39.0				
	CASC	$795,246	12.8				
Other:	Co-ed	21,798,385	12.1				
	All	124,467,828	15.3				

FIGURE 8-1

CASC are receiving all the support that could be expected from their own natural constituencies: churches, trustees, individual friends, bequests, alumni, and communities. The great opportunity for advance is with the corporations and foundations; in these two categories, CASC colleges are at the bottom of the list.

Why these colleges are at the bottom of the list for corporations and foundations is hard to understand for two reasons. First,
as has been mentioned, they are a good buy on the educational
bargain counter of today. That is, they can be expanded at
relatively lower costs than the price of building new institutions
or developing those which already have expensive plants and
equipment. Second, CASC and all small colleges represent an
unusually attractive investment opportunity for those who are
looking for alternatives to Federal aid. Whereas the financial
needs of the large state and private institutions may have to be
met by taxes and Federal aid because they are beyond the means
of private enterprise, the capital and operating costs of the
small colleges are well within the scope of foundations and
corporations. From the standpoint of the foundations this is the
chance to back experiments or pet projects in religion, the arts,
human relations, community services, teaching methods, and
curriculum changes. This is the opportunity for the relatively
small private investor to make his influence felt effectively in a
variety of ways in small institutions scattered all over the country.

A strong precedent has already been established in this direction. During the fiscal year ending June, 1956 (before CASC had
started to function as an organization), the fifty-two colleges then
holding membership in CASC received 5.8 million dollars from
a number of private sources: 1.3 million from religious groups;
3.4 million from bequests; $500,000 from corporations; $300,000
from foundations; and $250,000 from their alumni. Sixteen mem-
bers reported over $100,000 apiece in gifts. The distribution
showed that twenty-six colleges received from both their churches
and alumni, sixteen from both foundations and corporations, and
eleven from all four groups.

CASC Alumni Support

For the fiscal year ending in 1956, thirty-five CASC colleges
reported their alumni support to the American Alumni Council.
A sampling of the results of fifteen representative colleges is
shown in Figure 8-2. The range in total returns was from
$2,610 to $63,750; the total was $173,904; the average, $11,600.

NOT MUCH MONEY...	BUT	...A LOT OF LOYALTY	
COLLEGES	DOLLARS	COLLEGES	PER CENT
Findlay	$41.61 $11,591	Nat.Coll.	56.5% 438
AAC AVG	41.50	Upland	35.0 445
King's College	37.77 5,490	Gordon	32.7 849
Gordon	34.30 29,120	Prov-Barr'n	30.5 450
Robert's Wes	33.87 7,825	Salem	30.1 753
Westmont	30.49 12,162	Huntington	27.8 250
Steubenville	26.19 2,200	Westmont	24.0 399
Wm. Penn	26.15 8,891	Steubenville	19.4 84
Milton	21.02 9,248	Marlboro	17.6 26
Huntington	17.75 4,438	Milton	17.6 440
Ricker	16.51 1,899	AAC AVG	17.4
Salem	14.83 11,167	Robert's Wes	15.4 231
Morris Harvey	12.24 63,750	King's College	12.9 148
Marlboro	9.50 247	Wm. Penn	11.4 340
Prov-Barr'n	7.26 3,266	Findlay	7.3 272
Nat. Coll.	5.96 2,610	Ricker	3.8 115
TOTAL AVERAGE	$173,904 $11,600	TOTAL AVERAGE	5,240 350

FIGURE 8-2

It is clear from this bar graph that the average individual gift is below the national average; however, it is also clear that alumni loyalty, or percentage of donors to those solicited, is well above the national average for colleges in this category—private coeducational. In evaluating the results it must be borne in mind that many of these alumni are engaged in the ministry, teaching, nursing, and other low-paid service professions. It should also be remembered that several of these colleges are less than twenty years old, a fact which means that their alumni have not had time to accumulate substantial wealth.

At the Nasson Workshop in the summer of 1956, A. V. Wilker, trustee of the Union Carbide Educational Fund, told the CASC presidents that in evaluating a college one of the first things he would be interested in was its alumni support. "If your alumni have shown little or no financial interest in their college," he said, "it would be pertinent to know the reason why." Apparently Mr. Wilker was satisfied with his evaluation of the CASC colleges because five months later the Union Carbide Educational Fund made a grant of $500 to each of the then fifty-three members of CASC (a total of $26,500).

HOW HAS CASC HELPED TO MEET THE FINANCIAL CHALLENGE?

One of the four main functions of the executive office of CASC is to help with fund raising. This means providing information for the member colleges in their own individual efforts; but it also means raising funds for the projects and operations of the council as an organization, with indirect benefits for the entire membership. This assistance has been provided during the first two years of CASC's career in the following ways:

1. Studying corporation and foundation policies to identify likely prospects.

2. Preparing a handbook, *Small Colleges—An Untapped Resource,* for the information of prospects considering the support of CASC and its members.

3. Procuring the advice and influence of a board of advisers with interests largely in the financial field.

4. Organizing regional committees and promoting their activities with college-and-industry luncheons, lists of prospects, solicitation appointments, fund-raising literature, and office help.

5. Preparing and launching a campaign to raise 3 million dollars for faculty salaries to be distributed on a formula basis among all participating members.

The results of these efforts are reflected in Figure 8-3. It is worth noting that a number of these "blue ribbon donors" have made two or three gifts to CASC for its projects and operations, thus demonstrating satisfaction with their original investment.

Two important elements in the success of the council's effort have been "prestige gifts" and the group approach. The first prestige gift of $26,500, previously mentioned, came from the Union Carbide Educational Fund. This made it easier to procure the second of $82,000 from the Fund for the Advancement of Education. Following this lead, the United States Steel Foundation, Inc., Sears-Roebuck Foundation, General Electric Company, Esso Education Foundation, *Time* Incorporated, and many others quickly championed the cause of the small colleges. By September 1959, 35 donors had contributed $318,000.

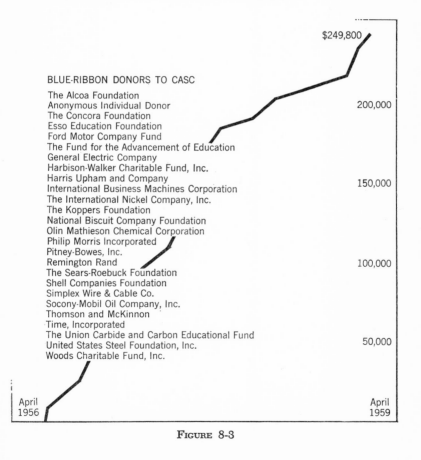

BLUE-RIBBON DONORS TO CASC

The Alcoa Foundation
Anonymous Individual Donor
The Concora Foundation
Esso Education Foundation
Ford Motor Company Fund
The Fund for the Advancement of Education
General Electric Company
Harbison-Walker Charitable Fund, Inc.
Harris Upham and Company
International Business Machines Corporation
The International Nickel Company, Inc.
The Koppers Foundation
National Biscuit Company Foundation
Olin Mathieson Chemical Corporation
Philip Morris Incorporated
Pitney-Bowes, Inc.
Remington Rand
The Sears-Roebuck Foundation
Shell Companies Foundation
Simplex Wire & Cable Co.
Socony-Mobil Oil Company, Inc.
Thomson and McKinnon
Time, Incorporated
The Union Carbide and Carbon Educational Fund
United States Steel Foundation, Inc.
Woods Charitable Fund, Inc.

FIGURE 8-3

One of the most outstanding contributions and examples of leadership was provided by the United States Steel Foundation. CASC received $10,000 from this source in the spring of 1957 and a second $10,000 in 1958. However, in addition to this, Westmont College and Piedmont College received $25,000 each; and a number of other CASC members received grants of $1,000 each. The effect of the $25,000 grant was dramatically demonstrated in the case of Westmont, which achieved regional accreditation shortly after receiving the U.S. Steel grant made for that specific purpose.

With respect to the group approach, CASC has found numerous doors open to a national organization which would not have been open to an individual institution—particularly a small one. This has provided many a CASC president an opportunity to tell the story of the small colleges (his own in particular) at a national level otherwise inaccessible to him. It has also meant that through grants made to the council as a whole the colleges in New England were able to share in the contributions of West Coast benefactors and vice versa.

HOW HAVE THE SMALL COLLEGES SHOWN INITIATIVE AND ORIGINALITY IN RAISING MONEY?

The point has already been made that the small colleges might be more impressive in their group impact on a problem than they were as small units. The originality, variety, and volume of ideas for fund raising show what has been done in local situations across the country. A number of such activities are reported here because, in many cases, other colleges could use them with slight modifications. They are presented under different headings according to the group involved or the purpose to be served.

Students

Eastern Mennonite College allows two extra days of Christmas vacation to its students, faculty, and staff. They use this time for voluntary solicitation of their parents, relatives, and friends and have sometimes returned to the college with as much as

$25,000 as a result of their efforts. Above and beyond the actual value of the donations received this scheme has had the additional merit of turning all its people into "salesmen" for the college—an excellent way to build internal morale and strengthen public relations.

Huntington College for a number of years has been successfully operating a student workday which is reported verbatim as follows by the student director of personnel:

In the fall of 1949, the student body petitioned the faculty to be dismissed from classes for one day in order to hire out to the community. The proceeds were to be used to purchase and install an electric organ in Davis Hall, where the four-days-a-week mandatory chapel sessions are held. "Since we have to attend chapel," someone unflatteringly remarked, "we might as well make it as enjoyable as possible."

The faculty not only acceded to their request but joined in the work crew. "Organ-ized Labor Day" was the catch-word slogan, and the students really sold it to the community. Jobs a-plenty were secured from leaf raking and window washing, selling apples, and polishing shoes to taking places in the assembly lines of the city factories and behind the counters of the stores.

The day was a success; the organ was purchased, installed, and dedicated to the memory of the students who had given their lives in World War II. The entire project was student: conception, organization, execution, and follow-up.

Since the first Work Day, the students have conducted six more. They have not made it an automatic yearly event, feeling that it takes a wanted goal to enlist the necessary enthusiasm and cooperation of the Student Union. The faculty takes no more than an advisory position in the projects; especially since the poorest returns from a Work Day came in response to a goal which the students felt was too strongly suggested by the college.

Following are the goals, together with the years in which Work Days were held: 1949—electric organ; 1950—paving of all campus driveways; 1951—furnishing the new library building; 1954—founding and equipping the new student lounge; 1955—finishing the student lounge; 1956—purchasing new audio-visual equipment with accessories and supplies.

The series has resulted in good public relations with the community . . . and excellent attention to detail by the various student administrations.

Gordon College reports that on a particular occasion its students raised $2,000 and donated many hours of volunteer labor for the construction of a tennis court. When completed, it was blacktopped, illuminated at night, landscaped, made adaptable for outdoor basketball, and made suitable for gatherings of a considerable number of people for special programs.

Northwest Christian College and *Madison College* are outstanding among the many CASC colleges to report the use of student labor in their building programs at great financial saving to the institutions. It is difficult to imagine this sort of student activity in a large college or university, but in a small college—especially a rural one—it appears to be appropriate and successful. The by-products in good campus morale and community relations are worth a great deal in addition to the financial contributions.

Alumni

Gordon College in 1948–1949 received $5,878 from its alumni; in 1956 it received $29,891. Two factors were involved in this dramatic increase: the inauguration of an alumni office with a full-time alumni secretary and the launching of a five-year capital gifts campaign. The well-equipped alumni office maintains appropriate files, sends a magazine to a mailing list of 2,500, sends out a variety of mailing pieces during the year, and leads the regional chapters in on- and off-campus activities climaxed by an alumni day in June. In recent years there has been a better than 35 per cent effectiveness of solicitation among all alumni and better than 42 per cent among graduates.

Roberts Wesleyan College has established a simple scheme which could be easily adapted to any college. It has signed up 300 alumni to contribute $5 a month regularly through the device of a coupon book about the size of a small checkbook. The result is $18,000 a year. Furthermore, the average annual gift of $60 is well above the national level.

Upland College indulged in a stunt which netted it $9,000

from its alumni in one evening. It happened this way: the president of the college arranged with Lever Brothers to have a gift of 300 cakes of Dove toilet soap "auctioned off" at an alumni banquet. The cakes of soap were lined up to form a "brick wall" across the front of the head table. Following a speech and other activities, the president and chairman of the alumni association sold the cakes to the audience on a scale of arithmetic progression. The first cake went for 10 cents, the second for 20 cents, the third for 30 cents, and so on; the three-hundredth cake sold for $30. The total amounted to $4,515. However, this was only half the story. It had been announced in advance that one of the trustees would make a matching gift of $4,500 provided all the cakes were sold. In effect, this doubled the value of everyone's contribution and provided all the incentive needed to reach the goal. The amazing thing was that the people involved formed the nucleus of a group which had just finished pledging $63,000 toward a $75,000 long-range goal. This fund-raising trick might not be suitable for Harvard or Columbia, but in Upland it worked like magic.

Upland has also used the novel idea of raising a million pennies from its students—sounds like a lot. It is a lot.

Milton College rings the bell. A publicity-conscious member of the staff persuaded the president to ring the chapel bell once for every extra $5 sent by an alumnus between June 15 and July 1. Two hundred and forty former students responded to this challenge, and the president with the help of several members of the faculty tolled the old bell for ten minutes. "Nothing like this has happened for years!" was the comment on Main Street.

Church Support

Dana College has arranged with the Evangelical Lutheran Church to double its support from $58,660 in 1955–1956 to $120,000 in 1956–1957 and again in 1957–1958 toward a goal of 1 million dollars for its development program.

Tabor College has worked out a plan for its Mennonite constituency to budget its support for the college to run between $80,000 and $100,000 annually over a five-year period.

Pikeville College reports that the Presbyterian Church has doubled its annual appropriation and is considering a challenge fund to boost the expansion program. In 1955 the women of the local church gave nearly $100,000 toward the new building to accommodate the unusual combination of a chapel and a science laboratory.

St. Joseph's College decided early in 1958 to attempt to raise $500,000 through a fund-raising campaign. This was the only fund-raising campaign ever undertaken in the history of the college. It ended during the last week of November, 1958. Expenses and fund-raising fee (to Commonwealth Consultants, Inc.) were estimated at less than 4 per cent of the total raised.

On the advice of the advisory board a firm of architects was retained during the spring of 1958 and professional fund-raising counsel was hired. It was decided that the appeal would be directed largely to the thirty-five Catholic parishes in Maine where the Sisters of Mercy either teach in parochial schools or conduct Confraternity of Christian Doctrine classes. A survey of these parishes was made during the last two weeks of May. No work on the campaign was done during the summer.

Actual organizational work on the drive began in the middle of September, 1958. Support was enlisted from the bishop of the Portland diocese and from twenty-nine of the thirty-five pastors contacted. A 20-page brochure was prepared and presented to the bishop and the twenty-nine pastors at a luncheon meeting on October 7, 1958. The importance of the college to the parochial school system was stressed at this time and throughout the campaign. St. Joseph's educates most of the state's parochial school sisters during summer sessions, when the enrollment amounts to about two hundred.

From October 7 to November 17 organizational work continued. State chairmen were enlisted, as were other chairmen on the state and parish level. Stories on the progress of the campaign appeared every week in the daily and Catholic press throughout the state. By November 17 all workers, down to the last team member in the most remote parish, were in the organization, which numbered some 3,500 men.

On November 19 the state kick-off dinner was held in Portland. Some five hundred pastors, parish chairmen, and state chairmen attended. The featured speaker was Richard Cardinal Cushing, Archbishop of Boston. The next night kick-off dinners were held in the separate parishes.

On Sunday afternoon, November 23, the parishes were solicited simultaneously. This solicitation produced $475,000. Special gifts and solicitation by mail of the college guild, alumnae, parents, and priests of the diocese have brought in another $100,000. The fund is expected to total $750,000 when all reports and gifts are in.

The campaign stressed the pledge system, with payments spread over three years, and memorials were sold, beginning at $120 and going up to $10,000. The success of the drive will make it possible for construction on the dormitory to begin in the spring of 1959.

Community Support

Ricker College has involved the leadership of its community in an unusual way. The local Rotary Club sponsored a "radio auction which lasted for three days, raised $10,000 for the college, and improved town-gown relations all around."

Tabor College, according to President Leonard Franz, "has conducted a community project to put a new gymnasium-auditorium on the campus." This has been one facet of a multi-pronged fund-raising program during 1958.

The city of Hillsboro, in the heart of the wheat and dairy country of Kansas, has a population of 2,500. There are a few industries, including Kansas's largest dairy products cooperative and two clothing factories.

On October 30 the college was host to three hundred business and professional people of the city and county at the sixth annual Tabor Booster Banquet, the kickoff for this fall's annual funds drive. Since last year all local contributions have been earmarked for the gymnasium fund.

The college received the full cooperation of the chamber of commerce. The group's president wrote a special letter which went to every resident of the city, outlining the value of the building project for the city. He appointed a committee of six, headed by the local postmaster who, together with six men from the college, contacted the business and professional men along Main Street.

The current drive has to date netted over $12,000 from eighty-two contributors. Added to $8,000 donated last year, the total Main Street giving toward this project is now $20,000. The city's merchants and professional people have indicated their intention to continue these annual budgeted contributions toward the gymnasium project for at least two more years.

A drive in the residential area and in the rural county area is set for early in the new year. A total subscription of $50,000 from local sources other than alumni and church constituency is seen as a distinct possibility by the end of the eighteenth-month-to-two-year construction period.

Hillyer College, now a part of the University of Hartford, provides an excellent example of the type of scheme in operation in many CASC colleges. It has an industrial advisory committee composed of seventy-five men representing major industries in Hartford. At periodic dinner meetings, they discuss their needs and the way in which the college can help to meet them. The college employs a man to give all his time to calling on industry; he never asks for money but rather what the college can do to help solve industrial problems. Thus the college is closely integrated with its community life and financial support is generated spontaneously.

The College of Steubenville has discovered that local labor unions represent a source of community support hitherto untapped. This college, located in the great coal and steel area of Pittsburgh and eastern Ohio, has turned the union device of the checkoff to its advantage. Local unions have agreed to allow employers to deduct 25 cents a week from the wages of those union members who are willing and turn over the proceeds to the college for capital investment.

Mount Marty College made a survey of the amount of money spent by its girls, faculty, and parents annually in the city of Yankton. With this information the college approached business firms asking them to contribute to a newly established scholarship fund. The response was more than satisfactory.

William Jennings Bryan College found a unique way to capitalize on its association with CASC according to the following quotation from its president, Theodore C. Mercer:

In planning how to meet the need for raising $5,000 as a part of the CASC 1-million-dollar campaign, the first obstacle to overcome was getting an angle which would bring in the $5,000 so that it could be certified that the sum raised was a bona fide additional amount over and above what the college normally raises. This was not easy. First, we applied to a Chattanooga foundation and received $500 instead of $5,000. Then it was decided to send a letter with an accompanying descriptive folder to five hundred persons, asking each person for $10.

Those selected to receive the appeal were those donors who had not given within the past year or two. I kept strictly away from those whose gift cards showed a regular pattern of giving. This was done so as not to hurt the prospect of the regular gift program of the college. Even in a mailing list of several thousand names, it was not easy to select five hundred people of whom you could feel reasonably sure that they would give $10 each.

The next task was the preparation of a brochure that would convey the solicitation idea in a verbally brief but visually effective manner. The theme of the brochure was *How* you *Can Help Raise $1,000,000.* The idea was developed under four heads: the Background, the CASC Plan, Bryan's Plan in the Campaign, What Can You Do to Help.

"The Background" section presented CASC and announced the plan for each CASC college to raise $5,000 for each of three years in order to be eligible to participate in the fruits of the national campaign. This section explained that Bryan had just recently adopted the Southern Association standards as its salary schedule and pointed out that the CASC requirement that the money be used for "improvement of instruction" fitted right in with Bryan's need. The section on "The CASC Plan" set forth the program of the 3-million-dollar campaign and described the plan for distribution. Section three, "Bryan's Part in the Campaign," explained the need for Bryan to raise $5,000 for each of three years; and the final section answered the question "What can YOU do to help?" by requesting each recipient of the letter to send in $10 as his or her part in the campaign.

The front cover of the brochure described the fund-raising project as "A Plan for Advancing Quality Education," and the back page carried the CASC slogan, "The Noise You Hear Is Progress." The back page also carried the information that the effort was carried on in cooperation with the Council for the Advancement of Small Colleges. The folder was prepared and produced in the college publicity and printing departments.

The brief letter sent out with the folder was autotyped. I personally signed each letter, however, and in the instances where I knew even slightly the individuals to whom I wrote, I appended a handwritten postscript touching upon some item I felt would be of personal interest to that prospective giver. Because the folder told everything, the letter was, of course, quite uninformative. A postage-paid envelope was enclosed.

The returns were interesting. Of course, we did not hear from everyone, but one man sent $1,000 instead of $10. Several sent $15, $20, $25; and a few who were not able to send the full $10 sent smaller amounts. One of the most encouraging facets of the response was the cheery manner in which the donors responded. Many wrote personal notes to accompany their gifts. The idea of "improving instruction," including the raising of teaching salaries and the striving for regional accreditation, seemed to receive wholehearted support.

Each giver was sent the official college receipt, along with a personal note of thanks. The campaign netted right at $7,000, and a few gifts are still coming in. The chief part of the campaign was restricted to one month. During this time the college also received a $3,000 unrestricted gift which we considered putting into the CASC fund; but we decided against that, thinking it would be better to go back to these people next year for a repeat gift rather than trying to say we raised two or three years' quota in one year. Besides the opportunity to present Bryan, the campaign enabled us to educate a good many people concerning CASC.

Morris College, according to this statement by President Reuben, was also able to "cash in on CASC."

After returning from the national CASC meeting last January in Miami, we decided to call together certain key persons in our state Baptist Convention and alumni association. The objective was to explain the nature and purpose of the national CASC financial drive and what our college was expected to do. In this meeting we made plans to raise the entire $15,000 in one big drive rather than in three annual $5,000 drives. We gave ourselves one year to raise this amount. A campaign committee was formed.

The campaign committee went to work immediately. It listed the following possible sources and areas of appeal: trustees, churches, alumni, and friends. Our big concern was how to raise our CASC money while conducting our usual drives for current operation and our present endowment drive. We stated clearly that (1) the CASC drive was for additional or "new money," (2) that it was to be used to strengthen our faculty, and (3) it represented an extra financial effort. We made special folders explaining the CASC 3-million-dollar drive. Offering envelopes were prepared, and several articles were carried in our local and state newspapers. We made two TV appearances during which the CASC drive was mentioned.

We decided to appeal to the trustees and churches first. The months of June, July, and August were set for the first phase of the drive. August 11 was selected as "Report Day." In our annual May trustee board meeting each trustee pledged to report $100. Our churches were sent CASC offering envelopes and other special literature which we had prepared and were asked to take a special offering. On August 11, $4,800 was reported. Later reports brought this amount up to $6,000 which we have deposited in a specially created "CASC Fund." An outstanding feature of our rally was a contribution of $1,300 from our summer school faculty and staff, who along with the students, each year select a project for which they raise money.

We expect to raise the $9,000 balance from our local community and alumni. A goal of $5,000 has been set for the Sumter community. The months of February and March have been selected for the drive. Already, our city council has promised to endorse this drive, and campaign workers are being recruited. The remaining $4,000 has been allotted to alumni areas which will report in the spring at a CASC victory drive dinner at which time we hope to complete the drive.

Foundation Support

Goddard College has been outstandingly successful in procuring grants for experimental projects from foundations. One example of this was an award of $30,000 from the Fund for the Advancement of Education for the purpose of inaugurating a program of independent study for first- and second-year students. Participants in this scheme, known as the Goddard College Study of Canadian-American Cultures, spend the months of January and February in a French-speaking Canadian community where classrooms and field experiences are realistically integrated and local television, radio, and moving pictures can be used to full advantage. Unusual experiments such as this illustrate one of the best ways for foundations and individual philanthropists to make their money go a long way in the small college.

According to President T. Leonard Lewis, *Gordon College*

. . . has made a successful effort in fund-raising and netted $68,448. A foundation approach for a specific purpose last year produced no results, but this year the same foundation responded. The objective was different and the presentation was different. Whereas last year I went alone, this year I was accompanied by a trustee. I stated the need for help from the academic side and the trustee made the pitch as a businessman. After the interview, I wrote out in detail our request which was favorably received by the foundation trustees and was followed by a conditional grant of $25,000.

At the time that the detailed request was mailed, the same request was presented in writing to another foundation which we had previously approached unsuccessfully. The trustees of the second foundation likewise responded favorably with a conditional grant of $25,000. This apparently encouraged one of our faithful friends who, without solicitation, informed me of a forthcoming gift of $18,448 undesignated.

Miscellaneous

Grand Canyon College has instituted a living endowment plan to underwrite current expenses. Income from endowment is sometimes regarded as evidence of financial stability by accrediting associations. However, it is difficult for a church-related college only ten years old to build up its invested funds to a point where the income will meet the operating deficit. Grand Canyon has a campaign to get donors to pledge, on a certificate, an annual gift equivalent to 4 per cent of a capital amount. The goal is $300,000 in capital which will pay the college a yearly income of $12,000 in the form of a living endowment. By Christmas of 1957—only a few months after the start of the campaign—the total pledged represented a capital sum of $180,000. Similar plans have been tried successfully in other CASC colleges.

Morris Harvey College has prepared an ordinary manila folder (printed in gold) to contain material about its bequest program. Included is a special brochure about the college with a message about the importance of leaving a will. The argument goes that no reasonable person would leave his home or his office for an extended trip without providing for things to be taken care of in his absence; how much more certain should he be that matters are properly arranged before he leaves on a one-way trip.

Northwest Christian College can point with satisfaction to a recent bequest of $400,000. This college has prepared a booklet, *Your Christian Will*, which tells the how and why of will-making and concludes with a message not to forget the instruments of the Lord, such as the college.

Northwest Christian College has also conceived the novel idea of "advancing the college a thousand miles at 10 cents a foot." There are 5,280 feet in a mile. Thus, if every dime advances the college by 1 foot, the goal of 1,000 miles equals $528,000. If enough people collect enough dimes, it's easy.

George Fox College has combined the request for testamentary gifts with the duty of tithing. It has shown that it is good business as well as good conscience for the donor to invest his tithes and then leave the invested funds together with the accumulated interest to the college.

When Milo C. Ross became president of George Fox College, he inherited a debt of $144,000, which was a major obstacle to regional accreditation. On January 18, 1957, the board of trustees voted to launch a debt-liquidation drive to pay off this sum by 1960. By September, 1958, the campaign had gone over $128,000 in cash and pledges. This was accomplished partly by special appeals to alumni but mostly by local "patriotism." The local chamber of commerce joined the college in its debt-reduction drive by including the college in its own industrial development campaign: "A Greater College for a Greater City." The chamber of commerce also assigned twenty-five speakers to the college speakers' bureau to tell its story to regional fraternal, civic, and religious groups; and it postponed until the fall of 1958 its own drive for membership funds in order that the college could solicit without competition.

George Fox College also has a living endowment plan through which individual subscribers pledge $25 a year. In 1946–1947, this fund brought in $6,093.93; in 1955–1956, it netted $35,584.15. In the meantime, the Friends Yearly Meeting had agreed to underwrite the fund to the extent of $20,000 annually.

Piedmont College employs an annuities plan whereby an individual turns over his funds to the college for investment. He receives a guaranteed income of more than 4 per cent at a specified age—usually sixty years—and the principal reverts to the college on his death. Piedmont also uses a "gimmick" known as the "Buck-a-Month Club" to encourage small donors to buy brick for the new building.

Marlboro College in Vermont conducts an undergraduate forestry program. It has rented a number of acres for a Christmas tree plantation, the rent to be paid in a percentage of harvested trees. Donors who give the college more than $50 receive in acknowledgment a free quart of maple syrup from the college's own trees.

St. Francis College in Brooklyn received a check for $2,000 representing $400 each for five of its graduates employed by the First National City Bank of New York. This is a reminder that small colleges of all kinds should do everything to take advantage of the many programs to match alumni gifts which are now conducted by major industries.

A number of CASC colleges have received grants from the International Nickel Corporation. Nasson College received a grant of $5,000 from the Kennecott Corporation. These are two industries that have responded to the particular appeal of the small non-regionally accredited college which was doing an outstanding job in education and efficient administration.

William Jennings Bryan College reported a successful "gimmick" in persuading the local city of Dayton to donate all the pennies collected from its parking meters for one week.

Sacred Heart College in Wichita was successful in "fining" all of its women graduates a penny an inch around their waistlines and their husbands a penny a pound. This made quite a sizable Christmas collection!

The College of Steubenville hit upon the idea of using the Living Endowment plan for a women's club, but had the problem of working out the plan.

In February and March, 1957 [according to President Egan] we interviewed fifty women, who represented a cross section of the community, and proposed our plan to them. They liked the idea but were very much opposed to having officers and regular meetings which would take up too much of their time.

Following their ideas, we inaugurated the plan in April, 1957. The plan is very simple in its operation, but very effective in its results as support for the college. A woman may become a member of the women's club by making a minimum donation of $5 each year, which would be equal to the income from a permanent endowment of $125,000. Each one is welcome to give as much as her means permit. The only obligation other than the annual contribution is securing a new member each year.

We, on our part, call one meeting a year, which is more in the nature of entertainment and a general get-together. We encourage members to bring guests who are prospective members to the affair. At the meeting we review the achievements of the year and ask each member to solicit a new member for the club, or to submit names to us. There is no way the membership can be increased except through the actual cooperation of the charter members.

For charter members this coming year will be the third year

of giving, and we can pretty safely assume that they will continue to give each year as a general practice. Their contributions thus far have been gratifying.

Mathematically speaking, if each member enrolls a new member, the enrollment of the club is doubled. This is an ideal situation which we do not expect, but we are fortunate in increasing the enrollment by at least 100 new members each year.

Our office informs the members of the activities of the college and of the women's club throughout the year. Correspondence to prospective members is handled by our office, but we use the names of the women who have submitted them as sponsor members.

This is a source of revenue that we had not received formerly, but which we believe is truly worthwhile and will produce satisfying results over the years.

SUMMARY

This chapter has had two main purposes: (1) to show the position of the small colleges relative to the national trends in fund raising, and (2) to show what the small colleges have been able to do for themselves, both through group action and by individual effort. The following conclusions appear warranted:

1. The disadvantages of Federal aid loom larger than the advantages for the small colleges.

2. Foundations and corporations could make their support unusually effective in the small colleges.

3. Through their combined and individual efforts the colleges of CASC have demonstrated an unexpected amount of financial strength and have shown considerable originality and initiative in solving their own financial problems.

4. The small colleges are using their natural constituencies— churches, alumni, and local communities—to great advantage.

Chapter 9

TRANSITION FROM NONACCREDITATION
TO ACCREDITATION

HOW CASC MEETS THE CHALLENGE OF ACCREDITATION

CASC has no quarrel with the principle of accreditation. It agrees that it is necessary for society to have some form of regulation of education at all levels, just as it is necessary to have police protection against crime and laws to protect the public against fraud and deception in the manufacture and sale of food and drugs. It agrees that this function can be performed better on a regional basis and by voluntary organizations than on a national basis and by Federal agencies. According to its constitution, a member of CASC must be "a college officially committed to and presenting evidence of an active program for early acceptance into the regional association."

CASC has tried to take a sane and sensible position on this subject. On the one hand, it has been sympathetic toward the problems of its members, toward their feelings of frustration and disappointment, and also their feelings of satisfaction when they have achieved accreditation. CASC was never intended to be a pressure group to force the hand of the regional associations or anyone else. It was started as a service organization for the improvement of its own members so that they would deserve and receive full recognition. They regard accreditation not as an end in itself, but merely as a stepping stone on the path of progress toward *advancing quality education*—a path which they would be treading regardless of the regional associations.

The way in which CASC has helped its members to meet the challenge of accreditation has been to operate its program for *advancing quality education*. This has already been stated in such detail, either explicitly or implicitly, that at this point it is sufficient merely to mention that it has included workshops and conferences on improvement and experimentation in curriculum, student-testing services, consulting services, business management studies, and fund raising. This has all been financed from the dues of the members or by grants for special projects from corporations and foundations.

CASC has helped to meet the challenge of accreditation in still another way. Before CASC was organized, the regional associations were dealing with an ill-assorted, unorganized number of individual institutions which might or might not have worthy programs and which might or might not have serious ambitions for accreditation by way of the long and rocky road of self-improvement. Since the advent of CASC, the regional associations have been able to deal with a responsible organization with professional leadership and reputable endorsement—an organization which by the terms of its constitution was dedicated to the same broad principles as those underlying regional accreditation. In other words, CASC has become a sort of "association to accredit the nonaccredited college" or more accurately a feeder organization for the regional associations and the other national groups whose membership is based on the criterion of regional accreditation.

In the October 25, 1958, issue, the *Saturday Review* ran an article entitled "Ford's $260,000,000 College Grants: What Happened." [1] The writer enumerated all the wonderful benefits to education resulting from this magnificent gesture by the Ford Foundation. However, one point went unmentioned, i.e., the formation and the work of CASC. This was a direct result of the fact that these "forgotten colleges" had been left out of the Ford grant. It does not seem to be stretching the point too far to say that unwittingly the directors of the Ford Foundation tossed the challenge of accreditation to all the non-regionally accredited colleges and that those which organized to help themselves formed CASC to meet this challenge. It is important to remem-

[1] Olga Hoyt, "Ford's $260,000,000 College Grants: What Happened," *Saturday Review*, October, 1958.

ber that when CASC was established, in spite of the numerous committees, commissions, workshops, research projects, etc., carried on by various groups, there was no single association dedicated to these two needs: the small college and regional accreditation. CASC filled this gap.

VIEWPOINTS ON ACCREDITATION

"I'd rather be good than accredited," said one CASC president in a moment of inspired oratory. Of course, what he meant was that he would still rather be both—good and accredited. In his case, the requirements of the regional association were being enforced so literally that in order to become accredited the college would have had to abandon its strongest reason for existence—a unique service to its supporting constituency. Furthermore, it would have been forced to undertake unreasonable expense to duplicate a service to its students which a neighboring accredited institution was already providing on an exchange basis. Under these circumstances, the remark of the CASC president makes a good deal of common sense and should represent a challenge to the regional association to reconsider its position in terms of the institution involved and in terms of the needs of higher education today.

In writing to a fellow college president whose institution had recently received membership in its regional association, one CASC president wrote, "Congratulations on your accreditation. Now that you have this obstacle out of the way, you can go on being the kind of college you have wanted to be all along."

These are fighting words and yet they are not hard to understand as coming from an idealist who had been knocking his head against a stone wall for many years—a wall which seemed to him to constitute an unreasonable barrier in the path of true progress.

A. V. Wilker, former trustee of the Union Carbide Educational Fund, has expressed himself in these words:[2]

[2] A. V. Wilker, *College and University Business,* January, 1959.

There was a time when I accepted accreditation without question as indicating that accredited colleges were good and acceptable and those that were not accredited were not. Closer association with colleges and universities developed during the last four or five years has changed that concept, but instead of bringing clarification, the final result has been confusion. I have almost come to the conclusion that accreditation and the method of carrying out accreditation have about passed the limit of their usefulness.

In one instance I am told a college is not accredited because its library contains fewer than 50,000 volumes. Yet, in looking through the statistics in the 1956 edition of *American Colleges and Universities,* I find there are a number of accredited colleges with libraries of fewer than 50,000 volumes, among them one that has recently reached the status of accreditation with only 1,300 volumes.

In another instance I am told that a certain college could be accredited provided it managed to get together an endowment of $500,000. In another instance the figure was 1 million dollars. Yet well-known colleges and universities of all sizes and kinds and reputations have little or no endowment. As a matter of fact, the *World Almanac* lists fewer than four hundred colleges with endowments in excess of 1 million dollars. This means that many hundreds of colleges have income from such sources of less than $40,000 per year—a relatively small percentage of the total required. . . .

Too, I am told that faculty-student ratios play an important part in the accreditation of a college, yet I find that these vary by tenfold. And while I am on the subject I may as well declare myself to the extent that to me the percentage of Ph.D.s making up the faculty is not necessarily the measuring stick of the excellence of the teaching done there. . . .

We all wish we could develop criteria that would be the true measure of scholastic excellence because, in the ultimate analysis, the test of the pudding is in the eating. By that I did not mean what the catalogue contains or claims but what kind of an education the graduates take with them when they leave. Buildings, grounds, equipment, and endowments are not necessarily an assurance of higher scholastic endeavor.

In spite of these statements, Mr. Wilker told the CASC presidents assembled at the Nasson Workshop in August, 1956, "Whether you like it or not, the lay mind does not understand the true meaning of accreditation, but it does accept it as a measure of scholastic excellence."

If Mr. Wilker's point of view is out of date or based upon misinformation (as is claimed by some of his critics), it is at least widely held by executives in foundations and corporations. If there has been a radical change in this position in recent years, then the regional associations have an obligation to inform the public and the colleges and to set the record straight.

No matter how much discouragement CASC colleges may have endured, no matter what feelings of resentment they may have harbored along the way, it is none the less true that they are very glad when they have acquired accreditation. This general feeling is reflected in the three following typical statements:

> The assurance came on March 13, as the crowning achievement of long preparation, adjustments, attainment of goals, and prayer, as the Western College Association granted accreditation to Westmont College, which brings natural recognition in the educational world. For this we shall not cease to praise Him. It is a tribute to His guidance and faithfulness. There was, and is, rejoicing among students, alumni, and friends as they have heard the good news, assuring graduates of the opportunity to enter graduate schools as well as making transfers to other colleges and universities readily acceptable.
>
> Roger J. Voskuyl
> President of Westmont College

> Morris Harvey has looked forward to this day for quite some time. We consider it a very important step in the development of a greater institution here, but we do not consider it the end of our journey. We are now in the process of developing a five-year program which, if successfully achieved, will make Morris Harvey one of the outstanding small colleges of America.
>
> Leonard Riggleman
> President of Morris Harvey College

Thanks sincerely for your message of congratulations on our accreditation. We are proud to have attained this coveted goal, and grateful for your interest and the help of CASC. Surely CASC can be proud of its record this year in graduating so many members through accreditation.

C. C. Madsen
President of Dana College

It seems appropriate to conclude the first section of this chapter with some words from William K. Selden, executive secretary of the National Commission on Accrediting. Ever since the first CASC meeting in Chicago and the first workshop at Nasson, Dr. Selden has been a wise and helpful friend to the council and its members.

At the Chicago meeting, Dr. Selden reported to CASC presidents that aside from their regional status, the similarities between the "recently accredited" colleges and the "not quite yet accredited colleges" were more striking than their differences. Their enrollments, for example, were approximately the same. The majority were church-related. Their average age was seventy-five years; they were distributed on a wide geographic basis. They were predominantly non-tax-supported and their greatest problems were financial.[3]

And yet [according to Dr. Selden] the tangible importance of accreditation is not limited to the area of college finance. Accreditation is now included among the requirements for an institution to become a member of the Association of American Colleges or the American Council on Education. It is among the requirements for institutions whose alumnae may be eligible for membership in the American Association of University Women. With rare exceptions, only accredited institutions are on the approved list from which nominations can be made for membership in the American Association of University Professors. Accreditation also exerts a positive influence on the status of a Federal employee under the United States civil service regula-

[3] William K. Selden, "Accrediting—What Is It?," *Bulletin of the American Association of University Professors,* vol. 42, no. 4, pp. 629–630, winter, 1956.

tions, where status depends on whether the individual is a graduate of an accredited or a nonaccredited institution. In a similar way, the accreditation of programs of study in such fields as architecture, dentistry, engineering, law, medicine, optometry, pharmacy, and veterinary medicine plays an important part in the process of obtaining the required state license to practice one of these professions.

On the positive side [according to the constitution of the National Commission on Accrediting] accrediting agencies have often been instruments against inadequately prepared professional practitioners; they have aided licensing authorities and facilitated the transfer of students; they have been helpful to students and parents seeking to identify sound institutions; they have aided institutions in withstanding improper political or other noneducational pressures; and they have stimulated broad consideration of educational problems and issues of more than local concern.

On the other hand, in seeking conformity to rigid definitions of physical facilities; in urging disproportionate expenditures for selected programs; in demanding standardized educational practices or standards that have little or no educational significance; in imposing on educational programs the judgments of professional groups; in defining the extent or scope of educational programs regardless of the wishes of the constituencies of educational institutions; in judging the desirability of administrative organization without regard for pragmatic consideration of effectiveness, and in making other determinations which properly lie within the jurisdiction of the faculties, administrations, and governing boards of colleges and universities, accrediting agencies limit, and endanger the essential freedoms of the institutions. Noncompliance with the imperatives of accrediting agencies not only endangers the welfare of the institutions, but also penalizes students who, because of the nonaccredited status of their institutions are barred from service to society.

QUESTIONS ON ACCREDITATION

CASC has enjoyed excellent relations and fine cooperation from all six regional associations ever since it started. One evidence of this was the invitation from the National Commission on Accrediting to submit a list of questions to be considered in a study of accreditation. Here is what CASC wants to know.

Is accreditation a hindrance to educational experiment?

How much importance is attached to the performance of students on recognized national tests?

How should financial stability be defined today?

How much attention is given to such matters as the age of a college, the size of its enrollment, its admissions policies, the qualifications of its faculty, the efficiency of its business management, and its aims or educational philosophy?

How much importance is attached to clear evidence of growth or progress in a desirable direction?

How much consideration should be given to a college's capacity for expanding its program and facilities to accommodate more students?

These questions stem from a genuine concern among CASC colleges with respect to the policies, practices, and long-range implications of the system of accreditation as it now exists.

CASC members are aware of the difficulties of judging "a good college." They are aware of the stigma which can come from "nonaccreditation." They do not suggest any relaxation of accreditation standards. On the contrary, they are trying to do everything possible to meet and exceed these standards. They are pleased with the recent shift in emphasis away from statistical evaluation of an institution and toward an appraisal of the quality of its program and the performance of its students. They invite the regional associations in the interests of all higher education to help break President Hurley's famous *vicious circle*— "You can't get accreditation without money, and you can't get money without accreditation."

Any college seeking accreditation has a long list of practical "how-to-do-it" questions beyond the scope of this chapter. Most of these questions can be answered from the offices of the various regional associations. The *Manual of Information about Recognized Accrediting Agencies* prepared by the National Commission on Accrediting, 1785 Massachusetts Avenue, N.W., Washington 6, D.C., offers a practical starting point. This contains a great deal of information about the purposes and requirements of the six regional associations as well as a number of professional accrediting agencies. The National Commission on Accrediting also has a long bibliography on the subject of accreditation. A condensed excerpt from one table in the manual is included here in order to indicate the range and variety of practices among the six associations, particularly regarding visits and expenses.

STATISTICAL STUDY OF SEVEN ACCREDITED COLLEGES

What has been said up to now should have made it fairly obvious that from an over-all national viewpoint accreditation is a complicated business, affected by local and regional cross currents and subject to numerous and various interpretations. CASC has conducted enough informal studies of its own membership to be quite sympathetic with problems confronting the regional associations. For example, it is almost impossible to select six simple criteria—such as enrollment, age, value of plant and endowment, faculty salaries, test scores, and student costs—and then find even half-a-dozen colleges that can be matched sensibly against these standards and rated from one to six. This observation leads to the conclusion that, although regional accreditation is good in principle, in that it encourages all colleges to meet certain minimum standards, it is also dangerous, in that it provides foundations, corporations, prospective students, and the general public with an extremely questionable device for measuring the true worth of a college. In case there is any doubt about this observation, CASC reports the following results of a study of its first seven members to receive regional accreditation.

By March, 1958, seven members of CASC had been accredited by three of the six regional associations: New England, North Central, and Western. Is there any pattern of statistical conformity evident among these seven newly accredited colleges? Here are some general observations: not one had fewer than 150 students; not one was less than eighteen years old; not one had a plant and endowment worth less than $500,000.

Out of curiosity the CASC office selected seven more colleges

TABLE 9-1

Regional associations	Number on accrediting team of visitors	Costs of initial accrediting visit	Fee to team members in addition to expenses	Annual dues
Middle states	5–75, including representatives of professional agencies	$150–$250, plus costs of visiting team and duplicating report	$100 for chairman only	Jr. colleges, $50 Sr. colleges, $100–$150
New England	3	Application fee of $75	None	$50
North Central	2–4	Jr. college, $500 Sr. college, $600	$40 per day for 3 or 4 days	Jr. colleges, $65 Sr. colleges, B.A., $135 M.A., $235 Ph.D., $335
Northwest	6–25, plus representatives of professional agencies	Costs of visiting team and duplicating report	None	Jr. colleges, $50 Sr. colleges, $75–$225
Southern	2–5	Jr. college, $300 Sr. college, $400	$50	Jr. colleges, $50–$60 Sr. colleges, $75–$225
Western	5–10, plus representatives of professional agencies	$350–$500	None	$150–$300

from its membership list which matched the seven newly accredited members as closely as possible on ten points. The two profiles are given in Table 9-2.

TABLE 9-2

Seven newly accredited		Seven nonaccredited	
Average full-time enrollment	372	Average full-time enrollment	430
Average age	54	Average age	61
Average number of Ph.D.s	12.5	Average number of Ph.D.s	10
Average cumulative GRE scores	2,500	Average cumulative GRE scores	2,650
Average tuition and fees	$425	Average tuition and fees	$480
Average faculty salaries	4,250	Average faculty salaries	4,066
Average value of plant and endowment	1,740,000	Average value of plant and endowment	1,420,000
Average gifts 1957	142,000	Average gifts 1957	65,500

Type of control:

Catholic	2
Protestant	2
Interdenominational	1
Independent	2

Type of control:

Catholic	3
Protestant	2
Interdenominational	1
Independent	1

Regional associations:

North Central	5
New England	1
Western	1

Regional associations:

North Central	2
New England	2
Middle States	2
Southern	1

An examination of these figures reveals that in comparison with the seven newly accredited colleges, the seven nonaccredited were 13 per cent older, that they took 15 per cent more students, that these students were taught by faculties with 20 per cent fewer Ph.D.s, that faculty salaries in these colleges were 6 per cent lower, that the performance of the students on the area tests of the Graduate Record Examinations was 6 per cent better, that more students were accommodated in institutions with 20 per cent less investment in plant and endowment, and that for the last fiscal year these colleges acquired 55 per cent less in total gifts. These percentages are illustrated in Figure 9-1.

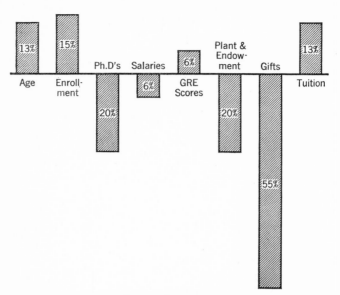

FIGURE 9-1. Seven Nonaccredited Colleges Compared to the Seven Recently Accredited Colleges, in per cent.

The nonaccredited colleges should be very much encouraged. This suggests the thought that if their brothers in CASC "have made it," they stand a good chance of success too. Furthermore, at least a dozen more colleges in CASC not included in either of these two lists would match these profiles so closely as to be indistinguishable.

Two features of these profiles warrant comment. One is academic quality; the other is financial strength.

If the regional associations are interested in encouraging and promoting academic quality, as judged by student performance on the area tests of the Graduate Record Examinations, then CASC has seven more colleges not included in any of the above lists, which average significantly higher (8 per cent) than those in either profile. Interestingly enough these seven high scorers on the tests have an average investment in plant and endowment of $700,000 (40 per cent) less than those just accredited, an average enrollment which is less by 78 students (21 per cent), a tuition which is higher by $200 (47 per cent), and an average age which is younger by seven years. Figure 9-2 is a graphic presentation of these figures.

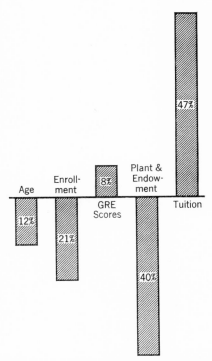

FIGURE 9-2. Seven Nonaccredited Colleges with Highest GRE Scores Compared to the Seven Recently Accredited Colleges, in per cent.

In case the regional associations are interested in plant and endowment, then CASC has still seven more colleges not included on any list mentioned so far in which the average amount in plant and endowment is $1,147,000 (65 per cent), greater than in the newly accredited colleges and in which the average annual gifts are $31,200 greater than for the newly accredited colleges.

The colleges in this group, oddly enough, had the poorest performance on the Graduate Record Examinations, the smallest average enrollment (262) of any group mentioned so far, and the lowest tuition—only $371. Their average age was only two years more than the average for the newly accredited group. Their position is reflected in Figure 9-3.

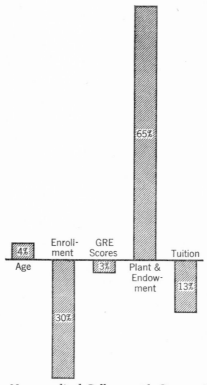

FIGURE 9-3. Seven Nonaccredited Colleges with Greatest Plant and Endowment Values Compared to the Seven Recently Accredited Colleges, in per cent.

None of this is reported in criticism of any of the regional associations. On the contrary, CASC is pointing out that the problem fo how to pick a good college is extremely complicated.

It would be wrong to conclude that "no matter how good you are, you can't win." It would be right to conclude that careful analysis of one's strengths and weaknesses is essential to true progress. This thought should give courage to those colleges in a stage of transition from nonaccreditation to accreditation.

EXPERIENCES REPORTED BY RECENTLY ACCREDITED COLLEGES

Time Involved

College A. A faculty committee was appointed in 1947–1948. In 1949, a consultant made a study of the college following the plan of the official survey. The first application was made in 1954 and denied in 1955. Another application was made in 1957 after many of the suggestions from North Central had been followed out. Accreditation was received in March, 1958. Total time— approximately ten years.

College B. The first self-study was made by a faculty committee in 1951. A more complete self-study was submitted to the North Central Association in 1952. The third and final self-study was started in the fall of 1956 and submitted to the North Central on June 28, 1957. The entire faculty was involved. Consultant service was used. Accreditation was received in March, 1958. Total time—approximately seven years.

College C. Founded as a junior college in 1927, this institution became a four-year college in 1942. The decision to apply for North Central accreditation was reached in August, 1954. In 1954 and 1955, curriculum and catalogue revisions were made. In 1955–1956, weekly faculty meetings were led by various members on discussions of all aspects of the purposes and program of the college. During 1956–1957, the college made the formal self-study required by North Central. Copies of the self-study were distributed to the student officers who led the whole student body in a review of the purposes and program of the college. Final steps were as follows: October, 1957, approval of self-study; November, 1957, submission of completed survey schedules; January, 1958, examination by official visitors; February,

1958, examiner's report to North Central; March, 1958, accreditation granted. Total time—approximately 3½ years.

College D. This had been a four-year college. It became a junior college and then returned to four-year status. Accreditation had been sought in 1948 but denied. The next self-study was started in 1953. This was followed by a second self-study and a self-survey. The entire faculty, administration, and board of trustees were involved. Consultant service was used. Accreditation was received in March, 1958. Total time—approximately five years.

College E. Self-study with a consultant in 1955–1956 was followed by a formal visit from accreditation committee in February, 1957. Report was submitted to the committee in March, 1957. Action was postponed and several recommendations were made. A supplementary report was submitted and accreditation was received in March, 1958. Total time—approximately three years.

Self-Studies

All colleges reported self-studies involving all members of the faculty, participation by administration and trustees, and in one case by students. Usually two or three studies were made. Consultant service was used in every case and found valuable.

Political Pressures

All colleges reported no political "pull" or pressure applied either by them or against them.

[One president said] The pressures that did exist were chiefly from invidious comparisons made by people because we were regionally nonaccredited. . . . Other [accredited colleges], so far as I know, have always treated us with complete fairness and courtesy.

[Another president said] We noticed no political pressures whatsoever. There was some concern on the part of a few members of the committee as to our religious position, but upon conference and explanation in detail, we found that the question was not raised at all at the last meeting.

Greatest Obstacles

College A. The greatest obstacle was lack of money. It was Dr. Hurley's vicious circle all over again—no accreditation without money and no money without accreditation. No objection had been raised to the educational program although a reduction in courses, an improvement in counseling, an increase in faculty salaries, and a change in admissions procedures had been recommended. Lack of accreditation had proved to be a hindrance in recruiting students as well as in securing financial support. A recent change in administration with some newly created offices had also caused the examiners some concern. Money was needed for additional dormitory and classroom facilities. (Finances.)

College B. The greatest obstacle we had to overcome was related to bents, biases, prejudices, and traditions among the faculty. . . . The most difficult task in the whole accreditation process was the education of the faculty in order to enable them to see the importance of the entire educational program and the relative importance of the various departments along with the entire college program. (Faculty.)

College C. The greatest obstacle was lack of financial stability. . . . Out of financial inadequacy grew neglect of such areas as faculty salaries, physical improvements, and the building of instructional aids. In recent years, the support has increased surprisingly and significantly from all sources and promises to continue. (Finances.)

College D. Our greatest obstacle was inadequate library facilities. With the procurement of the government loan and the United States Steel grant of $25,000, the way has been paved to move out of the dining hall and make available an area of 5,000 square feet for library purposes, whereas before there had been only 1,800 square feet. (Library.)

College E. When an organism is growing, no one thing need be the greatest obstacle, while many things may be handicaps. This college had all the needs of a growing institution: a new plant, more full-time and fewer part-time faculty members; a greater enrollment of students to justify curricular and financial expansion. (Rapid growth.)

In reply to a questionnaire in May, 1958, forty-five colleges

reported obstacles to accreditation as follows: financial insta-
bility (35), inadequate facilities (25), size (18), inadequate
faculty (21), too few A.B.s in liberal arts and too many vocational degrees (6), age (7). Of these, twenty-nine had had consultants on their campuses, but their replies did not differ from
the others.

Lack of accreditation was held to be a serious block in building up enrollment by thirty-five colleges. The trouble lay not
with the students but with their parents and with guidance
counselors. In the ten cases where it was not a factor, there
were strong church affiliations.

Assistance from CASC

All the colleges testified to the assistance received from CASC.
Two mentioned "the general improvement of the climate across
America toward the unaccredited colleges" which made "the
accrediting associations more aware of the potential of the nonaccredited schools." This is what Dr. Wilson M. Compton has
called "increasing the visibility of the small colleges." All mentioned the stimulation and encouragement received from such
activities as the CASC student-testing program, the workshops,
the fellowship with others facing the same problems, and the
additional incentive "to keep studying, keep plugging, keep
pushing." One mentioned specifically the inspiration received
from talks given at CASC meetings by professional consultants.
One mentioned the financial support from foundations and
corporations.

THE GREAT TRANSITION

There were once two caterpillars sunning themselves on a
branch when a butterfly zoomed by. Said the first caterpillar to
the second in some dismay, "You could never get me to go up
in one of those things!" But he did.

In review, several things must be expected during the transition from nonaccreditation to accreditation. First is a substantial period of time—anywhere from three to ten years—depend-

ing upon such factors as size, financial stability, type of program, necessary buildings, and academic standards.

Any transition stage involves two or three self-studies. Apparently these studies are conducted more rapidly and successfully under the guidance of an experienced consultant. Such studies should involve the entire college as much as possible and should be related closely to the specific requirements of the particular regional association.

It is not uncommon during this process to experience delay, frustration, and discouragement. These feelings can come from a number of sources—internally, from faculty members too slow to change; externally, from secondary schools, other colleges, and the community; from the general growing pains of a young institution, and financially, from corporations and foundations with policies against contributing to nonaccredited colleges.

The same tide raises all boats. Just as all colleges have been helped by the efforts of the Council for Financial Aid to Education in alerting the public to the importance of supporting higher education, so have nonaccredited colleges outside the membership of CASC benefited by the general publicity generated by CASC. However, the CASC colleges themselves have received the greatest benefits from their own organization which has served as their spokesman, friend, and honest critic. There are, believe it or not, worse things than being non-regionally accredited. It would never do to minimize the importance of this status. However, lack of it does not mean that all is lost. There are still young people to be educated, money to be raised, communities to be served, and jobs to be well done by dedicated people—all with or without accreditation. Perhaps the most important lessons that CASC colleges have learned in recent years are the importance of a conscientious effort to improve their own programs and the importance of sticking by their ideals and serving their own constituencies to the best of their abilities regardless of accreditation. Regional accreditation does not appear so formidable when it is regarded as the bottom step rather than the top step of the ladder which you are hoping to climb anyway.

It is important to mention in this connection the effect of the financial support received from a number of the country's leading industries. The United States Steel Foundation took the lead in this case by its grant of $25,000 to Ohio Northern College. This "seed money" induced other contributors to add their support. In a short time the college had acquired sufficient funds to meet the needs which only money could supply. This speeded up progress toward accreditation. This same thing happened in the case of Northland College a year later and in the case of Westmont College (a CASC member) in the third year. During recent years, U.S. Steel has given $22,500 to CASC for its general operating funds and about $150,000 to nonaccredited colleges.

One of the most significant contributions both morally and financially—to the whole problem of accreditation was made by the Fund for the Advancement of Education. The Fund made grants amounting to $82,000 to CASC in order to underwrite a national student-testing program and two workshops. These two workshops and the Michigan workshop with its implications for business management have already been described in this book.

COOPERATION FOR ACCELERATION OF TRANSITION

CASC must acknowledge gratefully all the assistance, both tangible and intangible, which the nonaccredited colleges have received in the last few years from many sources—foundations, corporations, national educational associations, regional associations, and influential friends.

In the best interests of all higher education, it is of the utmost importance for this type of cooperation to be continued and expanded.

Here is an idea for cooperation in order to accelerate the transition. This is a four-cornered situation. On corner A stands a large university or prestige college. On corner B stands a large foundation and a cluster of corporations. On corner C stands a small nonaccredited college. On corner D stands the regional association. Now, who makes the first move? They are all shy.

The university considers it beneath its dignity to extend a hand to its smaller and less fortunate neighbor. The foundations and corporations are looking to the university for leadership. They want to support only the best—by definition at least regionally accredited. The small college is sensitive; it too has its pride. The association would be willing to extend some help informally in the way of consultant services and invitations to annual meetings but not enough in the way of associate membership to be of substantial help in solving the problem.

So while they are all standing around staring at each other, nothing happens. Here are four suggested moves—one for each. It is not important which comes first.

The big university should offer to "adopt" the small college. It could then refer its surplus of well-qualified applicants to the small college. It could "lend" one or two of its most distinguished professors to the small college on a part-time basis to strengthen the academic program. It could make available some of its high-priced services in guidance, testing, and vocational placement, public relations, and consultant service in a number of areas, including business management. In exchange for these services, the small college might run various courses on an experimental basis for the big college. It could even serve as a practice teaching center for young liberal arts doctoral candidates who want to go into college teaching. In this case, the big university plays the role of the grateful beneficiary; the students receive a better education; and everybody wins.

In the meantime, the regional corporations come to life. They provide money to improve the existing physical facilities of the small college. They give it some secondhand office equipment. They provide some surplus scientific equipment. They offer assistance from some of their technical personnel. They offer part-time or summer jobs to the faculty and students. In exchange for these benefits, the small college conducts courses in secretarial training, business management, public speaking, accounting, industrial relations, or a host of other subjects to meet the needs of local industry and the local community. The small college reaps the tremendous advantage of financial support and business advice. The business wins local friends and customers and acquires a training ground for its future employees and managers. In addition, it enhances its public relations with the traditional American practice of the big helping the small. Again everybody wins.

All this time the leading local foundation is putting up the cash and consultant service to try out its pet experiment on a small scale in the small college at much less cost than that required in a bureaucratic, overorganized, gigantic institution. The small college receives the benefit of services otherwise far beyond its means and its prestige goes up. Again everybody wins.

While all this is happening, the regional association promotes one of its main purposes—the improvement of higher education for all. The way to improve education most is where improvement is needed most—in the small nonaccredited college. So it joins the party, and now the small college has three foster parents all cooperating to help set it on its feet. What does the regional association do? It extends associate membership to the nonaccredited college. By so doing it does not relax its standards for full membership in the slightest. However, it does give recognition to a college which is working and making progress toward the same goals for which the association stands. This recognition removes the curse of nonaccreditation, makes it more respectable for the foundations and corporations to give their support, and shares the responsibility for approval with the large university. The small college gains in stature and the regional association wins acclaim for helping to develop an underdeveloped institution. Again everybody wins.

This is the way to do it. It is the American way. Cooperation and mergers are familiar terms in both education and business. In very plain words, it is time for the American educational world to stop crying crisis over bulging enrollments, inadequate plants, low faculty salaries, and a shortage of teachers, scientists, and engineers when it has over one hundred small non-regionally accredited colleges scattered across the country capable of improving and expanding at extremely low costs.

If there is a real crisis and not just a fake one, then the secret formula for the solution of the problem is:

(Nonaccreditation + Cooperation) Acceleration = Accreditation

CONCLUSION

In conclusion it is well to recall the labels, slogans, and catch phrases which have characterized CASC—"The Noise You Hear Is Progress" . . . forgotten college . . . Operation Bootstrap . . . untapped resource . . . advancing quality education.

These are fighting words. They are not expressions of complacency. They reflect the attitude of a group of determined men and women with a cause to fight for and a will to win. However, there is nothing belligerent in these phrases. The emphasis is upon self-help and improvement. In fact, one of the outstanding characteristics of the group has been the desire of its members to do two things: preserve their independence and at the same time contribute to the main stream of education and coordinate their efforts with those of the recognized leaders in the field.

In today's world which is characterized by the "organization man" and the "man in the grey flannel suit" the great opportunity and great potentiality of the small college is to promote the independence of the individual. In this regard the colleges of CASC are providing a fine example to all of *how the small college meets the challenge.*

Appendix A

CASC BOARD OF DIRECTORS

President

K. DUANE HURLEY

President, Salem College
Salem, West Virginia

Vice-president

JOHN Z. MARTIN

President, Upland College
Upland, California

Secretary-Treasurer

ROGER C. GAY

President, Nasson College
Springvale, Maine

REGIONAL REPRESENTATIVES

Middle States

LEYMON W. KETCHAM, Assistant to the President

The King's College
Briarcliff Manor, New York

ELLWOOD A. VOLLER, President

Roberts Wesleyan College
North Chili, New York

New England

BEAUMONT A. HERMAN, President

Western New England College
Springfield, Massachusetts

C. WORTH HOWARD, President

Ricker College
Houlton, Maine

North Central

FRANCIS J. DONOHUE, President

St. Mary of the Plains College
Dodge City, Kansas

ARTHUR L. HEDRICK, Business Manager

Oakland City College
Oakland City, Indiana

Northwestern

ROSS J. GRIFFETH, President

Northwest Christian College
Eugene, Oregon

MILO C. ROSS, President

George Fox College
Newberg, Oregon

175

Southern

JOHN R. MUMAW, President
Eastern Mennonite College
Harrisonburg, Virginia

A. A. PAGE, President
Pikeville College
Pikeville, Kentucky

Western

ROBERT L. COX, President
Los Angeles Pacific College
Los Angeles, California

ROGER J. VOSKUYL, President
Westmont College
Santa Barbara, California

(Term expired June 30, 1959)

ROYCE S. PITKIN, President
Goddard College
Plainfield, Vermont

DEAN E. WALKER, President
Milligan College
Milligan College, Tennessee

Staff

Alfred T. Hill, Executive Secretary
The Council for the Advancement of Small Colleges, Inc.
1818 R Street, N.W., Washington 9, D.C.

Paul L. Zens
Staff Associate

Dottie M. Staples
Administrative Assistant

Appendix B

A DIRECTORY OF CASC COLLEGES

The following pages present descriptive and statistical material about seventy-one CASC colleges. Fifty-two of these make up the charter membership; thirteen joined CASC after April, 1956. These sixty-five are the colleges dealt with in the foregoing pages.

Six colleges joined CASC in the spring of 1958; each of these is marked with an asterisk in Appendix C. The twelve colleges which received regional accreditation after joining CASC are marked with a dagger.

The paragraphs about the colleges, which are arranged alphabetically, give some of the highlights of the history, program, and campus life of each college, and its admission requirements. They contain the most recent information available. Some colleges may have made slight changes in their fees, programs, or admission requirements since this book went to press.

ALDERSON-BROADDUS COLLEGE
Philippi, West Virginia

> Accredited by the North Central Association of Colleges and
> Secondary Schools, March, 1959.

Located 25 miles southeast of Clarksburg, this college enjoys a small-town environment. It is a coeducational Baptist-affiliated liberal arts institution. The physical plant includes a new dormitory to house 150 girls, gymnasium with a seating capacity of about 1,000, a music hall, and an observatory equipped with a Spitz planetarium. The college has a library of 47,000 volumes.

Broaddus Hospital is an integral part of the campus. It has a capacity of 106 beds and provides training opportunities for nursing, medical, and radiological technology students. The college offers two summer sessions totaling ten weeks. Admissions: 15 units; a minimum of 10 units should be in English, social studies, natural science, mathematics, and/or foreign language. Additional units may be in any subjects the high school accepts toward graduation. Plant and endowment: $2,907,661.

BUTLER COLLEGE
Tyler, Texas

In addition to its program in liberal arts, Butler offers courses in teacher preparation. It is characterized by a religious emphasis. Education is made available at low cost, and financial aid is provided through work opportunities and scholarships. Plans are under way for a new library to accommodate 40,000 volumes. Admissions: 16 units; required—English 3, history 2, mathematics 2, science 1; elective—8. Plant and endowment: $382,000.

CEDARVILLE COLLEGE
Cedarville, Ohio

Located in southern Ohio near Columbus, Cedarville has been granting baccalaureate degrees since 1887. It is a Baptist college of liberal arts where individual judgment and action are encouraged and developed. Majors are offered in Bible, education, English, social science, history, music, and science. Teaching fields in addition to majors include languages and physical education. Admissions: 15 units; required—English 3, mathematics 2, history 1, science 1; elective—8 units with a concentration in academic subjects. Plant and endowment: $500,000.

CHAMINADE COLLEGE
Honolulu, Hawaii

Chaminade is the only four-year private college in the Hawaiian Islands. It is also the youngest CASC college, having been founded in 1955. The curriculum is built on three areas of concentration: liberal arts, business administration, and education. The college has a very generous scholarship program; 40 per cent of the freshmen who entered in 1958 received financial aid in some form. Plant and endowment: $1,416,945.

DANA COLLEGE
Blair, Nebraska

> Accredited by the North Central Association of Colleges and Secondary Schools, March, 1958.

Students are drawn from eighteen states and Canada. Graduates have had an excellent record of success, and Dana has received many unsolicited statements from deans of graduate schools regarding the high quality of the preprofessional and undergraduate training of its students. The college offers a unique liberal arts reading course using a selection of two to four books each semester. Faculty members conduct small informal discussion groups based on the reading. Dana offers a good liberal arts training in an atmosphere of steadfast adherence to Christian ideals. Admissions: good character and ranking in the upper half of the graduating class. College preparatory program should emphasize English, science, mathematics, history, and social studies. Plant and endowment: $1,087,792.

DETROIT INSTITUTE OF TECHNOLOGY
Detroit, Michigan

This college has always tried to do a special job for two kinds of students: those who were unable to complete their education at the usual age and those who because of problems beyond their control had established doubtful high school records. DIT is nonresidential and in downtown Detroit. In the past several years it has had more than one hundred graduates on the payroll of the General Motors Corporation and many in Chrysler, Ford, and other companies. Programs are offered in arts and sciences, engineering, and business administration. There are a number of short courses in transportation, real estate, insurance, advertising, and general business. DIT attracts serious students who regard education as a means of preparing for a vocation as well as of acquiring a general cultural background. Admissions: graduation from high school plus special requirements depending upon the academic division applied for. Plant and endowment: $731,-343.

DOMINICAN COLLEGE
Racine, Wisconsin

This college offers liberal arts and professional training to young men and women who desire to profit from the advantages of a small college. It is the only four-year college in Racine, a city of about 80,000. Development plans currently under way will improve the facilities of the campus in the immediate future. The B.A. is offered, with fields of concentration in business administration, English, history, and mathematics. Other features include four-year programs in education, elementary and secondary, and in music, applied and music education; three years in premedicine; two years in predentistry and medical technology; one year in nursing. Admissions: 16 units; required—English 3, mathematics 2, history 1, science 1; elective—5 of the remaining 9 must be in academic subjects. Plant and endowment: $2,000,-000.

EASTERN MENNONITE COLLEGE
Harrisonburg, Virginia

The college is located in the beautiful Shenandoah Valley. It has recently attracted students from some twenty-two states and seven foreign countries. Judging from a self-survey and participation in a joint survey of all Mennonite colleges, the potential for an expanded enrollment is consistent with the national trend. The college's astronomical observatory has been selected as one of the observation (moonwatch) stations to track the artificial satellites being projected into the atmosphere. The college's science program includes an excellent offering in premedical training and the college hopes to erect a new science building in the future. Admissions: 16 units; required—English 4, mathematics 1, social science 2, natural science 1; elective—modern

language, additional science, and mathematics recommended.
Plant and endowment: $1,552,346.

EDGEWOOD COLLEGE OF THE SACRED HEART
Madison, Wisconsin

Accredited by the North Central Association of Colleges and
Secondary Schools, March, 1958.

The primary purpose of this college is to prepare teachers for
kindergarten and elementary grades. An outstanding feature of
the curriculum is insistence upon a strong liberal arts program.
Every student is required to take, as a preparation for her professional studies, certain courses in all major areas of the arts
and sciences. In its courses of teacher preparation, the college
is unusual in that methods are minimized and subject matter is
emphasized. Edgewood is a small, friendly college, a student
community where all students and faculty members know each
other. A new campus is being developed on the shores of beautiful Lake Wingra. In the fall of 1957, the students occupied the
new Regina Hall, with its 114 rooms and dining and lounge
facilities. The college has a new library with a capacity of 21,000
volumes. There is an excellent biological station and a new
campus school for the preparation of teachers for primary and
elementary grades. Admissions: 16 units; required—English 3,
mathematics 2, history 1, natural science 1, foreign language 2;
elective—of the other 7 units, at least 2 must be from these same
academic fields. Plant and endowment: $941,066.

EUREKA COLLEGE
Eureka, Illinois

This college enjoys a small-town environment 18 miles east of
Peoria in the fertile agricultural area of central Illinois. There
are twelve buildings on a 40-acre, parklike campus. Chartered
in 1855, it has developed an enviable list of distinguished alumni
and ranks second highest among all Illinois colleges in percentage of graduates listed in *American Men of Science* and fourth
in Illinois in percentage of graduates listed in *Who's Who in
America*. A distinguishing feature of this college is its intensive

study plan, which permits students to work exclusively on one or two subjects during each of the four 8½-week terms. Every class meets daily Monday through Friday. The library has 32,000 volumes. Most students earn part of their modest expenses on supervised jobs at the college. The college offers vocational guidance and operates a placement bureau. Admissions: 16 units; required—English 3 and other nonvocational subjects 6; elective —7 units. Plant and endowment: $989,079.

FINDLAY COLLEGE
Findlay, Ohio

This college of approximately three hundred students estimates it will double its enrollment by 1970. Findlay has been successful in preparation of teachers for elementary and secondary schools. It has an outstanding geology department. Since Findlay is a small institution, it seeks to foster person-to-person relationships between faculty and students and to emphasize personal counseling and individual classroom attention. Admissions: high school transcript, recommendations, and approval by admissions committee. Plant and endowment: $2,250,000.

FORT WAYNE BIBLE COLLEGE
Fort Wayne, Indiana

The college occupies an 18-acre campus in an exclusive residential area in southwestern Fort Wayne, near the center of the industrial Middle West. Students customarily attend from twenty-five states, including Hawaii, and five foreign countries. Ample scholarships and work opportunities are made available to those in need of financial assistance. The curriculum offers specialized preparation for the ministry, public school teaching, foreign missionary service, music, and Christian education. The college is accredited by the Accrediting Association of Bible Colleges, Indiana State Department of Public Instruction. Admissions: graduation from high school with acceptable record plus examination under special conditions. Plant and endowment: $1,250,000.

GEORGE FOX COLLEGE
Newberg, Oregon

In the last ten years, Oregon's school population has grown 189 per cent. The president reports that, "dollar for dollar ours is the most economical financing of any private college in the Pacific Northwest, thus making possible an adequate educational opportunity to Northwestern youths who could not otherwise have the advantage." Admissions: 16 units; required—English 3, social science 2, health and physical education 1, natural science and mathematics 2; 2 units in a single language required if a foreign language is selected. Plant and endowment: $1,013,185.

GODDARD COLLEGE
Plainfield, Vermont

The primary aim at Goddard is to help young men and women grow in maturity. This involves classwork closely related to the problems of the modern world and the needs of students. Each student works closely with his faculty counselor in carrying out his program. No formal examinations are given but both students and teachers carry on constant evaluation. All courses are elective to meet individual requirements. The student supplements his studies by two months of work experience away from college each winter in a nonresident term. Goddard emphasizes attaining intellectual maturity and carrying adult responsibility as fast as a student demonstrates his readiness. Grants from foundations have supported experiments and research devoted to studying and improving the conditions for learning, particularly through wider use of community and regional resources. Goddard has received financial support from the Fund for the Advancement of Education to conduct an experiment whereby students live for several weeks in the French cities of Canada. They study customs and ideas and thus make their language study a more meaningful experience. The college is beautifully situated in the Vermont hills. With a small student body, the atmosphere is informal. Admissions: high school graduation, satisfactory performance on college entrance examination, and personal interview. Plant and endowment: $373,267.

GORDON COLLEGE
Beverly Farms, Massachusetts

Gordon expects to double its enrollment by 1970. It is about 30 miles north of Boston on a beautiful campus site. It has a new and well-equipped library and a new dormitory. The long-range development plan envisions a sound and functional campus design. To the unusually intelligent and mature applicant, Gordon permits entrance at the end of the junior year of high school. Individuals of similar caliber who have excellent records their freshman year may be admitted to an honors program which gives adequate scope to their superior abilities. Admissions: 15 units; required—English 4 and 6 from foreign language, college preparatory mathematics, science, and social studies; elective—5 acceptable units. College entrance examination required. Plant and endowment: $1,936,905.

GRAND CANYON COLLEGE
Phoenix, Arizona

Grand Canyon is the only non-tax-supported college in Arizona. It is young and growing rapidly. Its teacher-training program for the public schools has been recognized as outstanding. The college expects to increase its enrollment from 400 to 1,400 students by 1970. It has recently completed a new library, which includes an unusually fine collection of the world's best classical records. Admissions: high school graduation or individual approval and examinations—16 units; required—English 3, mathematics 1, social studies 1, science 1. Plant and endowment: $754,000.

HILLYER COLLEGE OF THE UNIVERSITY
OF HARTFORD
Hartford, Connecticut

Accredited by the New England Association of Colleges and Secondary Schools, December, 1956.

Hillyer has the largest enrollment of any college in the CASC group, with a total of 5,000 students, and excellent prospects for doubling this number by 1970. At present Hillyer has no dormitories; the college conducts a thriving day and evening program and a "twilight" program from 4:30 to 6:30 P.M. for 1,077 teachers. The college has an active engineering science program for advanced students sponsored by the United Aircraft Corporation. Hillyer also has a varied and high-quality science program. It offers majors in mechanical engineering, electronic engineering, and industrial engineering. It gives the degree of B.A. in physical sciences, behavioral sciences, and science teaching, and the B.S. degree in business administration. It also offers the associate in science degree in mechanical engineering and in electronics. Through its technical institute, it offers an excellent three-year program for electronics technicians, a two-year program in instrumentation, and a one-year basic electronics program.

On Sept. 1, 1957, Hillyer became Hillyer College of the University of Hartford, through a merger with Hartt College of Music and the Hartford Art School. The college has recently acquired a site of 150 acres for a completely new campus in the northwest corner of the city. Plans call for the construction of a new science and engineering building, and a music and fine arts building within the next three years. Hillyer College is located strategically from the standpoint of future growth and development, both with respect to the number of students served and expanding cultural and industrial needs. Plant and endowment: $3,000,000.

HUNTINGTON COLLEGE
Huntington, Indiana

Now celebrating its sixtieth anniversary, Huntington is the only institution of higher education sponsored and supported by the Church of the United Brethren in Christ. Approximately 55 per cent of the student body come from the supporting church; about 50 per cent of the graduates go into teaching. "The graduates stand for the basic principles of a society and an economic order which preserve the rights of the free enterprise system. It is true to what stalwart citizens choose to call 'the American way of life.'" The college emphasizes close student-faculty relationships and offers wide opportunity for student participation in extracurricular activities. Generous scholarships, grants-in-aid, and work opportunities are available. The college has a good library and is engaged in a campus development plan. Admissions: 15 units; 10 must be in English, foreign language, mathematics, social studies, and science. Plant and endowment: $1,-060,000.

JOHN BROWN UNIVERSITY
Siloam Springs, Arkansas

John Brown University has a threefold educational objective: the development of the head, heart, and hand. These objectives are summarized in two slogans: "Christ Over All" and "America's First University of Vocational Specialization." The institution maintains a strong Christian emphasis. Financial assistance is provided by academic scholarships, "service scholarships," and loans. Students usually attend from thirty-five states and five foreign countries. The college has participated in the North Central study of liberal arts education for more than ten years. A new library and a new science building are recent additions to the plant. Admissions: 15 units; required—English 3, mathematics 2, American history 1, plus electives. Admission by examination permitted in some instances. Plant and endowment: $5,950,000.

THE KING'S COLLEGE
Briarcliff Manor, New York

From a total of 421 graduates since 1942, 236 have undertaken graduate study. The high scores made on the Graduate Record Examinations have been indicative of the success the graduates have met with in the graduate schools of more than fifty colleges and universities all over the United States, including such well-known institutions as Boston University, Columbia, George Washington, Johns Hopkins, Lehigh, New York, Pennsylvania, Purdue, Rutgers, Syracuse, and Western Reserve. In addition to the usual offerings of a standard liberal arts college, students may major in music education, physical education, and pretheology. Enrollments have been expanding, and the prospects are that the college will double its size by 1970. Its plant, providing the luxurious accommodations of a former resort hotel, is on one of the more unusual and beautiful campus sites in the country; it is within easy driving distance of New York City and surrounded by places of historic and literary interest. Admissions: 16 units; recommended—English 4, mathematics 2, foreign language 2, science 1, social science 2; elective—5. Plant and endowment: $1,425,551.

LAKELAND COLLEGE
Sheboygan, Wisconsin

Founded in 1862, this is one of Wisconsin's oldest privately supported church-related colleges. It is located at the edge of the kettle moraine country between Sheboygan and Elkhart Lake, a popular recreational area; sailing, fishing, hunting, skiing, and tobogganing are an integral part of campus and community life. The college has recently completed a modern library building and a new women's dormitory. Academic fellowship is congenial and stimulating. Although 50 per cent of its students come from the local area, many states and several foreign countries are represented among the others. For over twenty-five years, students and graduates have transferred with full credit to the University of Wisconsin, Marquette University, and other colleges and universities. Admissions: 15 units; recommended—English 4, foreign language 2, mathematics 2, social science 2, science 2; the remainder electives. Plant and endowment: $1,607,-848.

LA MENNAIS COLLEGE
Alfred, Maine

Founded in 1951 and conducted by the Brothers of Christian Instruction, this is one of the youngest colleges in CASC. Its secondary school teacher-preparation program is accredited by the state department of education. The summer session (with a registration of 135 students) permits the earning of a degree in less than four years. For the benefit of community students, all classes are held during the forenoon. The discussion method of teaching and frequent personal conferences with students are features of a highly individualized academic program. Admission: 16 units; required—English 4, mathematics 2, foreign language 2, science 1, social science 2; elective—5 in academic fields. The college will move to a new $1,000,000 campus in Canton, Ohio, in 1960.

LOS ANGELES PACIFIC COLLEGE
Los Angeles, California

Founded in 1903 by members of the Free Methodist Church as an academy for their children, Los Angeles Pacific expanded until it was chartered as a senior college by the church in 1954. Since then it has continuously increased its offerings in the liberal arts, in theology, and in the applied arts and sciences to young people of all Protestant denominations. Located in the fastest-growing section of the country, L.A.P.C. enjoys the cultural advantage of the Los Angeles area. In addition to providing on-campus work for worthy students, the college has arranged a cooperative employment plan with the industries of southern California so that students may earn most, if not all, of their college expenses. Admissions: 15 units; required—English 3, United States history and civics 1, science 1, mathematics 2, foreign language 2; elective—6. Plant and endowment: $1,230,000.

McKENDREE COLLEGE
Lebanon, Illinois

Founded in 1828, this is the oldest college in Illinois. In terms of continuous church control, it is the oldest Methodist college in the nation. Located just half an hour east of St. Louis, in the heart of a vast industrial empire, McKendree has launched an expansion program calling for 5.5 million dollars in capital funds and an increase in student body from 250 to 600. Preserving many of the best characteristics of the small church-sponsored college—but without sectarianism—it has graduated men and women who have won distinction in all walks of life. Primary interest is in the humanities, broadly defined, with nearly two-thirds of all students specializing in education and religion.

However, alumni who have entered scientific and technical fields have enhanced the reputation of their college. Admissions: 15 units; English 3, 8 distributed among mathematics, foreign languages, social sciences, and science; elective—4. Plant and endowment: $1,200,000.

MADISON COLLEGE
Madison College, Tennessee

This is a self-supporting institution. It draws its entire income from its hospital, farms, and industries. Every student is required to work a minimum of eighteen hours a week. Some students earn over 100 per cent of their expenses. The teachers have a true missionary zeal and are working for young people rather than for money. Many of the graduates have entered into employment looking for the good they could accomplish and not the money they could earn. The physical plant is in fine shape. All its buildings, including an excellent library, science building, demonstration school building, as well as classroom facilities, have been built by student labor. Emphasis is placed upon preparation for careers in nursing and medicine. Admissions: 15 units; required—English 3, mathematics 1, social science 1, natural science 1; electives—vary according to academic objectives. Plant and endowment: $1,329,995.

MADONNA COLLEGE
Livonia, Michigan

Accredited by the North Central Association of Colleges and Secondary Schools, March, 1959.

This is a young college in a fast-growing section of suburban Detroit. Located on a 320-acre beautifully landscaped site, the campus breathes an atmosphere of peace conducive to study and cultural refinement. It is accredited by the Michigan Commission on College Accreditation and approved by the Michigan State Board of Education. The current enrollment of approximately one hundred full-time students makes it possible to give attention to individual needs. As a Catholic liberal arts college, Madonna seeks to develop an intelligent, cultured, and religious woman who can share her riches with those in her family and community. Within the framework of its liberal arts program, the college offers professional or preprofessional preparation in such fields as elementary and secondary teaching, medical technology, home economics, business, social work, and journalism. Admissions: 15 units of high school work including two major and two minor sequences from English, mathematics, foreign language, social science, and natural science. Plant and endowment: $302,205.

MALONE COLLEGE
Canton, Ohio

Malone College was founded in 1892 to provide training for prospective ministers, missionaries, and Christian workers. In recent years, the curriculum has been expanded to offer courses in religion and philosophy, language and literature, science and mathematics, education and psychology, fine arts, and social science. In its new location on a beautiful 54-acre tract in the residential section of Canton the college has erected new buildings which form the nucleus of a plan for a four-year Christian liberal arts college. Through its expansion in buildings, facilities, and staff the college will be able to provide for an increased number of students who wish to prepare for a variety of vocations in a warmhearted Christian atmosphere. The college recognizes its dual responsibility of serving the interests of the Ohio Yearly Meeting of Friends Church with which it is affiliated and many of the educational needs of the local community. Students seeking admission must present evidence of graduation from an approved high school. Beginning in September, 1959, all applicants presented scores from the College Board Examinations. Plant and endowment: $1,200,000.

MARIAN COLLEGE
Fond du Lac, Wisconsin

Marian College exists primarily for women seeking to increase their education and to prepare themselves for careers of service. Students enrolling at the college may choose a regular liberal arts course or they may select a program preparing them for careers in education, nursing, and medical technology. Every student's program is implemented by a strong program in general education, and all four-year curricula lead to the bachelor of science or bachelor of arts degree. The college also offers a two-year curriculum in rural elementary education. The college proper, the school of nursing, and the school of medical technology are all on the same campus. The school for observation and practice teaching is within easy walking distance. Two other features characterize Marian College: the friendly spirit of a small college and emphasis on keeping student expenses at a minimum. A graduate of an accredited high school, who ranks in the upper half of her graduating class, who merits the recommendation of her high school principal, and who presents sixteen acceptable units is eligible for admission to Marian College. Plant and endowment: $800,000.

MARLBORO COLLEGE
Marlboro, Vermont

Founded in 1946 to provide the freest possible interchange of ideas between teacher and student, Marlboro has attracted a group of thoughtful and responsible students and enthusiastic teachers. About one-third of the members of the faculty hold the Ph.D. degree or its scholarly equivalent, but the major emphasis is on teaching. The heart of the curriculum is a group of general education courses which are followed by a comprehensive examination after two or three years of college work. Upperclassmen who have completed the examination have great freedom in planning their work in advanced courses and special projects. The success of Marlboro's educational program has been demonstrated by high student scores on nationally recognized examinations and acceptance of the college's credits by distinguished Eastern liberal arts colleges. A student "town meeting" runs the college community, and students are represented at faculty and trustee meetings. Plans call for rapid expansion in the next few years, but the college will remain small. Applicants for admission should seek a personal interview and should submit secondary school transcripts and scores of recent aptitude and intelligence tests. Plant and endowment: $240,000.

MARYMOUNT COLLEGE
Los Angeles, California

This is a liberal arts college located in suburban West Los Angeles. Students enjoy the city, including Hollywood Bowl programs, the Huntington Library, and Griffith Park Astronomical Observatory. The intellectual development of the Christian woman is the primary aim of the college. It achieves this by liberal and professional training in a spiritual and cultural environment, with ample opportunities for experience in living. Marymount College maintains programs of foreign study in Canada, France, Italy, Spain, and England. Scholarships, both full and partial, are awarded for scholastic ability, leadership, and artistic ability in the fields of theatre, music, and art. Awards are based on high school record and recommendation of the principal, competitive examination, and College Board Examinations. Admissions: 15 units; required—English 3, foreign language 2, mathematics 2, history 1, laboratory science 1; elective—6. Plant and endowment: $1,110,470.

MESSIAH COLLEGE
Grantham, Pennsylvania

Formerly a junior college, Messiah has been granting baccalaureate degrees since 1952. The college draws its students largely from its supporting denomination, the Brethren in Christ Church, but also from approximately twenty other denominations. It offers a two-year course in business, a two-year course in religion, and a two-year course in general education, as well as a special two-year nursing curriculum followed by a three-year term at the Harrisburg Hospital. Admissions: 16 units; required—English 3, mathematics 2, science 1, social studies 1; elective—9 units, with no more than 3 from vocational subjects. Plant and endowment: $1,025,000.

MILLIGAN COLLEGE
Milligan College, Tennessee

Founded in 1882, Milligan College is located in the mountains of northeastern Tennessee, in an area of increasing population and expanding industrial development—particularly in the plastics, textiles, publishing, paper-making, hardwoods, and mining industries. Milligan is coeducational and has an enrollment of four hundred students drawn from twenty-four states. About 80 per cent of its students are residential. It has modern buildings and an attractive campus. Specialties are offered in music, teaching, business, prelaw, premedical, preministerial, and pre-engineering. Admissions: 16 units; required—English 4, foreign language 2, history 1, mathematics 2, science 1; elective—6 according to the program desired. Plant and endowment: $2,413,-000.

MILTON COLLEGE
Milton, Wisconsin

Milton has been doing an outstanding job with its "student rehabilitation" program. For several years, the college has been taking as many as forty-five students who had had an unsatisfactory academic experience in larger colleges and universities. After reviewing their high school records and giving them an examination, Milton has admitted these students on probation and made a definite effort to put them into good academic standing. It has been successful with at least 75 per cent of this group, half of whom have chosen to remain at Milton rather than to return to larger campuses. Milton takes pride in its low student-faculty ratio, which provides for maximum personal attention. The college slogan is "Large enough to serve you; small enough to know you." The college enjoys excellent community relations and offers student aid and work programs of various kinds. Admissions: 15 units; recommended—English 3, mathematics 1, social science 1, natural science 1, plus electives in foreign language, mathematics, science, according to college program desired. Plant and endowment: $700,000.

MONTREAT COLLEGE
Montreat, North Carolina

Montreat provides one of the most scenic campuses in the country, situated on a lake in the heart of the Blue Ridge Mountains. It was founded as a part of the religious and educational program of the Mountain Retreat Association, a declaration of trust of the Presbyterian Church U.S.A. It is a center for year-round conferences sponsored by the association. A fundamental purpose of the college is the preparation of teachers. Admissions: 16 units; required—11 from English, social studies, mathematics, languages, and science.

MORRIS COLLEGE
Sumter, South Carolina

Morris College was established in 1908 by the state Baptist Educational and Missionary Convention of South Carolina for the Christian and intellectual training of Negro youth. The college is located in a beautiful town of 33,000 population in the eastern part of South Carolina. The college offers specialties in teacher preparation as well as a two-year terminal secretarial course. Admissions: 15 units; required—English 4, mathematics 2, history 1, science 1; elective—the remaining seven must be selected from an approved list. Plant and endowment: $1,306,-904.

MORRIS HARVEY COLLEGE
Charleston, West Virginia

Accredited by the North Central Association of Colleges and Secondary Schools, March, 1958.

Morris Harvey is located in an area of rapidly increasing population and rapidly developing industry. The college draws over 90 per cent of its enrollment locally and keeps its costs low. The college is operating in a beautiful plant with a long-range development program to make it one of the outstanding campuses of its region. In addition to a strong on-campus liberal arts program, Morris Harvey College offers extension courses, evening classes, and classes over TV and radio stations. Admissions: 16 units; required—4 in English plus a distribution of the balance among mathematics, science, history, foreign language, and a few electives. Plant and endowment: $3,750,000.

MOUNT MARTY COLLEGE
Yankton, South Dakota

This is the only four-year Catholic college for women in the state of South Dakota. Founded as a junior college in 1936, the college expanded to a four-year liberal arts college in 1950. The traditional claim of the college to be a "home away from home" makes it possible for Mount Marty to pride itself on the home and family atmosphere patterned on the Benedictine way of life, where personal relationships between faculty and students are maintained. Admissions: 15 units; required—English 3, mathematics 1, science 1, social science 1½, plus electives, only 4 of which may be in vocational subjects. Plant and endowment: $2,759,111.

NASSON COLLEGE
Springvale, Maine

Career training balanced by equal distribution in liberal arts courses is a distinguishing characteristic of the college's effort to shape its program to the needs of modern society. Nasson's extensive research program for several pharmaceutical manufacturers has won wide recognition. The college is located in the industrial heart of Maine, an area in which the population is increasing more rapidly than the national average. Currently under way is a development program to raise 1.5 million dollars, about a third of which is projected for endowment and equipment, and the remainder for new construction. Nasson has recently dedicated a new women's dormitory—an added attraction to its rapidly developing physical facilities. Admissions: graduation in the upper half of class from an approved high school. Plant and endowment: $2,071,348.

NATIONAL COLLEGE
Kansas City, Missouri

Located in a residential area 3½ miles east of the center of Kansas City, National College offers many opportunities for cultural and intellectual growth as well as advantages for developing a sensitive awareness of social problems. Having completed more than a half-century of service in the field of education, the college offers a distinctive program of training young men and women for Christian service leading to a bachelor of arts degree. It also has a work program designed to reduce the costs of room and board for resident students. National College draws students from all races, from nearly every state, and from many foreign countries. Admissions: graduation from an accredited high school or completion of 15 units of work and successful passing of an examination given at the college. Recommended units include: English 3, foreign language 2, mathematics 2, history or social science 1, laboratory science 1; elective—6. Plant and endowment: $2,166,972.

NEW ENGLAND COLLEGE
Henniker, New Hampshire

Founded in 1946, this is another of CASC's young colleges with an unusual program. New England operates on a plan whereby students can get the bachelor's degree in three years. Each term lasts thirteen weeks, and a three-hour course meets four times a week. Thus a full semester's work is covered in each term for each course. Because of this three-year plan, the college can produce needed graduates in liberal arts, business administration, and civil and contracting engineering in less time than is usually required. This college is located in a small town in a "typical" New England setting. Admissions: 16 units; required—English 4, mathematics 2, science 1, history 2, language 2; elective—5. Registration open for fall, winter, and spring terms. Plant and endowment: $200,000.

NORTHWEST CHRISTIAN COLLEGE
Eugene, Oregon

This is a low-cost college drawing students who are particularly interested in preparing for church vocations or in obtaining a general education with emphasis on Biblical and Christian disciplines. Attendance is largely from the Northwest. Students at Northwest Christian College may also take work at the University of Oregon upon complying with requirements for admission to that institution. The college and the university work in close harmony on arranging such programs of study. About 95 per cent of the students work part time to help defray their expenses. Student labor was used to help build a new library recently. Above 60 per cent of the men who graduate continue their studies in theological seminaries. Admissions: prospective students must have graduated from approved high schools or give evidence by examination of ability to pursue college studies. A minimum of 15 units of high school preparation or the equivalent required for admission. Plant and endowment: $1,330,000.

OAKLAND CITY COLLEGE
Oakland City, Indiana

Oakland City is located in a rural area. Costs are kept low to accommodate students from low-income families. By attending summer sessions students may complete work for their degrees in three calendar years. During the last year, the physical plant has been newly renovated and a completely new building with an auditorium and classrooms has been made available. Admissions: 16 units of acceptable credit from a commissioned high school or certification that the equivalent credit has been granted. Plant and endowment: $1,088,000.

OAKWOOD COLLEGE
Huntsville, Alabama

Approved by the Southern Association of Colleges and Secondary Schools, December, 1958.

Oakwood College is the outgrowth of the Oakwood Industrial School, founded in 1896 at Huntsville, Alabama, by the General Conference of Seventh-day Adventists. In 1916, the school became a junior college; it achieved the status of a senior college in 1944. The college property consists of 964 acres, at an elevation of 1,100 feet above sea level. A college-operated farm occupies 500 acres of the property. Oakwood College offers the bachelor of arts and bachelor of science degrees in biology, business, chemistry, education, English, history, home economics, music, and religion. Terminal courses are offered in prenursing, two-year business curriculum, and two-year Bible instructor's course.

Admissions: 16 units; required—English 3, algebra 1, mathematics 1, foreign language 2, American history and government 1, science 1; elective—7. Plant and endowment: $1,332,802.

OLIVET COLLEGE
Olivet, Michigan

Founded in 1844, Olivet is the second oldest college holding membership in CASC. It is related to the Congregational Christian Church but welcomes students of all faiths. Located in a growing area in the south central part of Michigan, it draws the majority of its students from that state. It is a liberal arts co-educational college and takes full advantage of the unique opportunities present in a small school for close faculty-student relationships. Emphasis is placed on preparation for graduate study. Admissions: graduation from high school or preparatory school. Students are considered on the basis of demonstrated academic ability, character, interests, and promise of future usefulness to society. Admission tests may be given in special cases. Plant and endowment: $3,000,000.

PAUL QUINN COLLEGE
Waco, Texas

Paul Quinn has a potential for doubling its enrollment by 1970. Sophomore and senior comprehensive examinations must be passed successfully before students may graduate. Sophomore examinations test comprehension of principles in the major areas of the general education program. Senior examinations refer to the student's general interpretation of basic knowledge in his major area of specialization. Admissions: by academic record— 15 units required; by examination; and by individual approval. Plant and endowment: $1,083,336.

PIEDMONT COLLEGE
Demorest, Georgia

"The trends of our day," according to the president, "have encouraged many young people to expect something for nothing from the government or from somebody else. At Piedmont we encourage young people to help themselves through our work-aid and scholarship program. Many of our students work on the campus, in the kitchen, dining hall, offices, library, and maintenance department." Over 80 per cent of the enrollment is from homes in the foothills of the Blue Ridge Mountains. The college is officially committed to the traditional American ideals of thrift, hard work, integrity, and free enterprise. Approximately 60 per cent of the graduates have become teachers. During the past few years, the college has built a new gymnasium and has made a good start on a new science hall. Admissions: school records or entrance examinations must show preparation and ability to do college work satisfactorily. Plant and endowment: $1,538,986.

PIKEVILLE COLLEGE
Pikeville, Kentucky

Pikeville claims recognition because it is doing a job that no one else is doing. It serves a region which, until the past twenty-five years, was quite isolated. Young people from the Kentucky mountains do not usually desire to leave home. A recent survey indicated that no other section of the country as heavily populated as this had so few educational opportunities. Since 1953, enrollment has increased over 100 per cent. The trend is sharply upward for the next few years. Ninety-five per cent of the students come from within a radius of 75 miles. The nearest comparable institution of higher education is 120 miles away. The college offers specialties in pre-engineering, premedical, teacher training, and prenursing programs. Admissions: 15 units; required—English 3, algebra 1. Plant and endowment: $939,012.

PROVIDENCE-BARRINGTON BIBLE COLLEGE
Providence, Rhode Island

Providence-Barrington is in a gradual stage of transition from its old plant in Providence to its new and beautiful 110-acre plant in Barrington, 9 miles distant. When completed, the college may be able to enroll at least double and possibly triple its present number of 500 students. This is a coeducational, interdenominational liberal arts college offering ten majors. Ten denominations are represented on its faculty of forty-one. Students represent between thirty and forty different church bodies. For some time, the college has been engaged in intensive self-study with a view to development in every area. The college has a library of 30,000 volumes, a unique collection of classical records and tape recordings, and an annual library budget of $15,000. Among the strong points of this college are its programs for preparing students for careers in nursing, teaching, social work, and Christian service. Admissions: 16 units; required—English 4 and foreign language, mathematics, science, or history 5. All candidates must give satisfactory evidence of Christian character, physical fitness, and proper attitude toward the standards and objective of the school. Plant and endowment: $1,450,000.

RICKER COLLEGE
Houlton, Maine

Ricker, "the College of the Northeast," serves particularly its county of Aroostook but welcomes to its campus young people from other areas seeking a program leading to a bachelor's degree at moderate cost. Courses are organized to give an associate in arts degree in prelegal, premedical, predental, prenursing, and secretarial science as well as the bachelor's degree in liberal arts and business administration. Special attention is given to those preparing to become secondary school teachers. Admission is on the basis of high school graduation from a program directed toward college entrance plus a recommendation from the principal. Plant and endowment: $1,026,822.

RIO GRANDE COLLEGE
Rio Grande, Ohio

Founded in 1876, Rio Grande serves a number of counties in southern Ohio, drawing 80 per cent of its students from within a radius of 50 miles and the rest on a national distribution. One of the strong points of this college is its low faculty-student ratio, which enables the faculty to give special attention to the students' personal as well as academic problems. Rio Grande College endeavors to encourage a Christian philosophy of life and to further democracy in education by making the college economically accessible to all who are capable of benefiting by higher education. Rio Grande is a liberal arts college, with special emphasis on a four-year educational program leading to a B.S. in secondary and elementary education. The college also specializes in pre-engineering, premedical, preagricultural, and predental programs. A foundation formed by a local corporation has recently built and furnished a girls' dormitory; students and community citizens assisted in the construction of a student center opened in 1957. Plans for a new administration-classroom building have been announced. Admissions: 15 units; foreign language not required, but fewer than 2 units of a foreign language will not be accepted toward the required units. Veterans accepted without high school credit if GED test result is satisfactory. Plant and endowment: $1,865,612.

ROBERTS WESLEYAN COLLEGE
North Chili, New York

Roberts Wesleyan College, a Christian institution of higher learning, is strategically located in suburban Rochester, a cultural and educational center of western New York. A strong academic program revolves about the liberal arts, with additional excellent programs in teacher education, business, music, religion, and collegiate nursing. The collegiate nursing program is Roberts-directed in cooperation with accredited hospitals in the area. Ninety per cent of the student body "earn while they learn" in a self-help program on campus, in a small plastics factory on campus, and in nationally known Rochester industries. Campus and plastics-company wages earned average $115,000 annually. Admissions: graduation from a recognized high school with average grade of C or upper three-fifths of class. The college entrance examination is required in some cases. The college administers selective tests throughout the four-year program under the special direction of a guidance director. Plant and endowment: $914,705.

SACRED HEART COLLEGE
Wichita, Kansas

The college was established in 1933 but was reorganized as a four-year liberal arts college in 1952. Sacred Heart is devoted to the higher education of the women in the local area, and although teacher preparation is stressed, a sound liberal arts curriculum is also offered. The campus comprises 80 acres and affords ample opportunities for recreation. A loan fund and a small number of assistantships are available to students who cannot meet ordinary expenses. Admissions: graduation from an accredited high school or the equivalent, with 4 units in English, 2 in foreign language, 2 in social science, 2 in mathematics, and 1 in laboratory science recommended. Students may be accepted provisionally in some cases. Plant and endowment: $1,656,777.

ST. FRANCIS COLLEGE
Biddeford, Maine

Started as a junior college in 1943, the institution became a four-year college in 1953 granting B.A. and B.S. degrees. St. Francis is a Catholic college but students of other faiths are welcome. The college is currently revising the scope of its majors in favor of a restricted core curriculum comprehensive enough to assure a rounded liberal arts education and yet limited to courses that can be handled successfully by the small college. St. Francis is trying to keep its total fees low in order to make its opportunities available to students of moderate means. It offers scholarships, financial aid, and work opportunities to help students who need to "earn while they learn." Concentrations are offered in business administration, accounting, classical languages, economics, education, English, French, history, mathematics, philosophy, and sociology. Admissions: 16 units; required —English 4, algebra 1, American history 1, plane geometry 1; elective—9. Scholastic aptitude test required in special cases. Plant and endowment: $1,055,582.

ST. FRANCIS COLLEGE
Brooklyn, New York

Accredited by the Middle States Association of Colleges and
Secondary Schools, March, 1959.

In 1956 the college inaugurated two new programs. The first
is known as the Brooklyn Historical Studies Institute. Its purposes are to make the student aware of the rich historical background of the local community and to awaken the local community to an awareness of the contribution of the college to local
life. The students are carrying on research under the direction of
an authority on the history of the area. The faculty will collaborate with the students in the publication of a final report. The
second project consists of an agreement with the Haskins Laboratory to carry on research in microbiology under renowned specialists in the field. The college conducts a very careful program
of guidance and screening for its students and offers remedial
work in reading and speaking. There is also a strong vocational
program with personnel bulletins, conferences, and consultant
services to steer students into fields where they will be most productive. This is a day college with no boarding facilities. It
offers premedical, predental, prelaw, and pretheological programs. Admissions: 16 units; required—English 4, language,
mathematics, science, and history 5. Students must have a 75
average and earn satisfactory rates on entrance examination.
Plant and endowment: $1,220,250.

COLLEGE OF ST. JOSEPH ON THE RIO GRANDE
Albuquerque, New Mexico

The College of St. Joseph on the Rio Grande is located just
outside the northwest city limits of Albuquerque—a metropolitan center with a population of approximately 175,000 and the
cultural and business center of the Southwest. The college is
affiliated with the Catholic University of America. Its credits
are accepted for full transfer value by all the nation's leading
colleges and universities. Many of its graduates have done ex-

ceptional work in graduate schools all over the country. This is a coeducational institution with an enrollment of 415 students. In addition to a full liberal arts program, the college offers journalism, drama, art, music, and athletics. The science division is especially strong, offering majors in chemistry, biology, and mathematics and a minor in physics. The department is staffed by four professors holding Ph.D.s. Professional degrees are offered in business administration and in education. Admissions: 15 units; required—English 3, mathematics 2 (with at least one unit in algebra), social science 2, laboratory science 1; elective— not more than four of the remaining units may be earned in nonacademic subjects. Plant and endowment: $1,774,000.

ST. JOSEPH'S COLLEGE
North Windham, Maine

St. Joseph's College draws 90 per cent of its students from Maine. It is located on a new and spacious campus in an area adapted to year-round sports. Many graduates have achieved outstanding success as teachers in public schools. Students are attracted by the pleasant, homelike atmosphere of the college. Admission: 16 credits; required—English 4, foreign language (ancient or modern) 2, social science 1, science 1, mathematics 2; elective—6. Plant and endowment: $2,180,000.

COLLEGE OF ST. MARY
Omaha, Nebraska

Accredited by the North Central Association of Colleges and Secondary Schools, March, 1958.

This college was founded as a junior college in 1923, became a limited four-year college in 1940, and a complete liberal arts college in the fall of 1955 when it was established in its new plant at a cost of over 3 million dollars. The college aims to give the young woman a fuller realization of her dignity, her duties, and her capacities as a woman. St. Mary also carries forward its general cultural program into the fields of professional education. Bachelor of arts and bachelor of science programs are offered as well as preparation for both elementary and secondary teaching, medical technology, medical record science, nursing, and home economics. Programs in music, art, and business education are also offered. Students come from fourteen states, largely Middle Western. Scholarships and grants-in-aid are available. Admissions: 16 units; required—English 3, algebra 1, geometry 1, history 1, science 1, language 2; elective—5 of the remaining units in academic subjects. Plant and endowment: $3,231,545.

ST. MARY OF THE PLAINS COLLEGE
Dodge City, Kansas

Founded in 1952, this is one of the youngest colleges in CASC and the only four-year college in southwestern Kansas. In fact, except for St. Mary of the Plains, people in this area cannot obtain education beyond the junior college level within 110 miles. The college has an excellent plant, well-equipped laboratories, and an outstanding faculty of twenty members who hold advanced degrees from fourteen universities. A feature of its strong music department is a carillon—one of two in the state of Kansas. The college is noted for its programs of preparation for teaching and nursing. The college has authorized a selection of twenty-five students for full-tuition scholarships on a basis combining merit and economic need, plus five to ten others involving these criteria but reserved for superior athletes. Admissions: 15 units; four years of English, mathematics (preferably algebra and plane geometry), social science (especially American history), and some laboratory science are recommended. Special examinations are necessary in some cases. Plant and endowment: $3,029,062.

ST. MEINRAD SEMINARY
St. Meinrad, Indiana

Founded in 1861, this is among the oldest colleges in CASC. The college offers a four-year liberal arts program and a four-year theological course in preparation for the priesthood. About 90 per cent of its students continue for advanced graduate study. One-third of its faculty holds earned doctor's degrees. The college library has 58,000 volumes and 250 current periodicals. The library budget averages $18,000 a year, and the facilities are used constantly by the faculty and students. In recent years, student applications have far exceeded the capacities of the college. St. Meinrad has a speech clinic to aid students with functional disorders in speech. It has a program for the preparation of secondary school teachers. One of its unusual features is a successful gardening project whereby the students are able to earn money to send directly for support of missions of their choice. The college has a 50-acre campus and is accommodated in beautiful buildings and grounds. Admissions: students are admitted under one of the three following plans: (1) graduation from St. Meinrad Minor Seminary High School Department; (2) graduation from other secondary schools with the proper scholastic preparation and from the upper half of the class or with a satisfactory score in the admissions testing program; (3) proper qualification and recommendation by their ecclesiastical superiors. Plant and endowment: $1,508,967.

ST. MICHAEL'S COLLEGE
Santa Fe, New Mexico

St. Michael's College is the second oldest educational institution in New Mexico, having been founded as a secondary school in 1859. In 1947 it became a four-year college on a new 123-acre campus. Three degrees are offered: Bachelor of Arts, Bachelor of Science, and Bachelor of Science in Business Administration. The college has a one-year intensive program in English for Spanish-speaking students from Mexico and from Central and South America. St. Michael's believes that a comprehensive extracurricular program is essential to develop well-rounded and completely educated young men. It is a member of the New Mexico Athletic Conference. Admissions: 15 units; required— English 3, social science 2, and a maximum of four in any one subject. Plant and endowment: $1,800,000.

SALEM COLLEGE
Salem, West Virginia

Salem College, as a part of its liberal arts program, maintains a strong department of teacher education and has been responsible for the preparation of a majority of the teachers in its part of the state. The curriculum also provides for special study in a wide variety of subjects, including Christian education and Bible, medical technology, business administration and secretarial studies, industrial arts, home economics, and music. An unusual feature is a course in human relations offered in cooperation with the American Humanics Foundation of Kansas City. This program is directed toward the development of youth leaders in such fields as scouting, Y work, church, and recreation activities. Among the college's distinguished alumni are the present senior Senator from West Virginia, the Governor of West Virginia, and two former presidents of the National Education Association. Admissions: 16 units; required—English 3 or 4, mathematics 1, 2 units in each of two other fields. Plant and endowment: $803,266.

SIOUX FALLS COLLEGE
Sioux Falls, South Dakota

Accredited by the North Central Association of Colleges and Secondary Schools, March, 1958.

Sioux Falls has recently introduced a program of general education, including such courses as basic science, introduction to fine arts, and communications skills. The present student body is drawn from eighteen states and four foreign countries. Graduates through the years have given a good account of themselves as products of a liberal arts education. Admissions: 15 units or GED test or by making up deferred high school units. Plant and endowment: $759,430.

THE COLLEGE OF STEUBENVILLE
Steubenville, Ohio

This college is in an area of greatly increasing population and is a community college under private auspices. Its regular curriculum is supplemented by night classes and part-time offerings. Programs include premedical, prelaw, and pre-engineering, business and accounting, education, history, political science, chemistry, biology, mathematics, fine arts, and economics, leading to a

B.A. or a B.S. degree. There are also two-year programs for associate degrees. Admissions: 15 units; required—10 in four of these fields: English, social science, foreign language, mathematics, or natural science; the others may be in any subject counted toward high school graduation. Examinations for special cases. Plant and endowment: $500,000.

TABOR COLLEGE
Hillsboro, Kansas

Tabor College is a small, but growing, liberal arts college in central Kansas. Support of the building program by loyal alumni and the Mennonite Church, plus corporate gifts, should make it possible to increase enrollment by 200 students within the next few years. Tabor's supporting church has inaugurated a five-year budgeted plan of support which nets the college approximately $90,000 annually. An increase of more than 100 per cent in donations from business and professional people in this area reflects the degree to which Tabor is accepted by the community it serves. A new library building valued at $200,000 was completed during 1957; designated gifts and an increased budget are adding significantly to the library's research facilities. The science division has moved into greatly enlarged and newly equipped laboratories. Plans are well under way for a student union, gymnasium, and men's dormitory. The student-teacher relationship is close, and education costs are kept low to aid the worthy student with limited means. Tabor's graduates have established a good record in many fields, with 40 per cent going into public school teaching. The college offers opportunities for expression in a well-planned program of intramural sports, intercollegiate athletics, forensics, and music activities. Admissions: 16 units with a concentration in such college preparatory subjects as English, history, mathematics, and science, plus the customary electives. Plant and endowment: $806,684.

UPLAND COLLEGE
Upland, California

Accredited by the Western College Association, February, 1959.

Upland is actively engaged in a building program. A survey

of community leaders indicates enthusiastic support of the drive. At Upland the mountains, ocean, and desert of the Far West become a laboratory for field trips and also provide exciting opportunities for fun and recreation. Students can find work in the local community. Admissions: 16 units; required—English 3, social science 1, foreign language 2, natural science 1, mathematics 2 (B average should be maintained); college aptitude tests required. Plant and endowment: $625,000.

WESLEYAN METHODIST COLLEGE
Central, South Carolina

Wesleyan Methodist has a well-established, regionally accredited junior college. The senior college, with a strong emphasis on Biblical studies, was established in 1955 to prepare teachers. Admissions: 16 units; required—4 in English, and 3 from languages, social studies, science, mathematics, or commercial studies.

WESTERN NEW ENGLAND COLLEGE
Springfield, Massachusetts

Western New England College offers a unique educational program in fields where there is a demonstrated national shortage. In performing its special function, it is alone among the schools of this geographical area. Formerly strictly a night school, it has opened a day program, thus greatly increasing its enrollment and doubling the utilization of its space. The college conducts the only school of law in Massachusetts outside metropolitan Boston. It is the only college in Massachusetts to offer baccalaureate engineering degrees in a night program. The college has always maintained close relations with the local industrial community. At present sixteen companies in the area are sending students to Western New England and paying their tuition. The college has recently acquired a 34-acre campus. In the near future, it plans to move from its present quarters in the YMCA building to new buildings. Admissions: 15 units; required—English 4, mathematics 2, United States history 1; for engineering and business curriculum—algebra 2, plane geometry 1, laboratory science 1. Plant and endowment: $1,337,371.

WESTMONT COLLEGE
Santa Barbara, California

Accredited by the Western College Association, March, 1958.

This college, located in an area with a rapidly increasing population, draws students from twenty-three states. In 1950, the enrollment was 219 students; in 1957, it was 373 students. The prospects are that it will double over the next few years. The physical plant is filled to capacity at present. Alumni loyalty is shown by the fact that over a two-year period 1,600 alumni have raised $16,000 to finish their special project of paying for a music practice room. Its new science building is equipped with an excellent telescope. The buildings and grounds comprise one of the most beautiful college campuses on the West Coast. Admissions: 15 units; required—English 3, foreign language 2, mathematics 2 (one in algebra), natural science 1, social science $1\frac{1}{2}$. Provisional students accepted in some cases. Plant and endowment: $2,430,000.

WILBERFORCE UNIVERSITY
Wilberforce, Ohio

Wilberforce celebrated its one hundredth anniversary in 1957. It draws students from twenty-nine states and seven foreign countries and is in an area where college enrollments are expected to treble by 1970. The college is actively engaged in a campus development program. Admissions: 15 units recommended; English 3 or 4, language 2, mathematics 2, physics 1, biology 1, American history 1, civics $\frac{1}{2}$. Plant and endowment: $2,198,226.

WILLIAM JENNINGS BRYAN COLLEGE
Dayton, Tennessee

Situated on an 82-acre wooded campus, Bryan enjoys a rural environment northeast of Chattanooga. There are nearby facilities for the study of natural science, including access to the Oak Ridge Atomic Laboratories. The college offers scholarships, grants, and loans to worthy students in financial need. The sports program is mainly intramural. Admissions: 15 units; required—10 from a distribution in English, foreign language, mathematics, and social studies; elective—5 from any subject credited toward high school graduation. Plant and endowment: $1,291,338.

WILLIAM PENN COLLEGE
Oskaloosa, Iowa

This is one of two Quaker colleges holding membership in CASC. The college is especially strong in preparation for teaching. Approximately 50 per cent of its graduates have entered this field. During the past six years, about 40 per cent of its alumni have gone on to do graduate work. Among its distinguished alumni it numbers eight college presidents and thirteen persons in *Who's Who in America,* including well-known educators, authors, physicians, social workers, scientists, and government officials. The college has a library of 37,000 volumes. It offers generous scholarships to qualified students. Students come from several states and foreign countries, with twenty-one different denominations represented. Admissions: 15 units; required—English 3 or 4, natural science 2, mathematics 2, modern foreign language 2, social science 2. Plant and endowment: $1,758,810.

Appendix C

MEMBERSHIP LIST

ALDERSON-BROADDUS COL-
LEGE †
Philippi, West Virginia

BUTLER COLLEGE
Tyler, Texas

CEDARVILLE COLLEGE
Cedarville, Ohio

CHAMINADE COLLEGE *
Honolulu, Hawaii

DANA COLLEGE ††
Blair, Nebraska

DETROIT INSTITUTE OF
TECHNOLOGY
Detroit, Michigan

DOMINICAN COLLEGE
Racine, Wisconsin

EASTERN MENNONITE COL-
LEGE
Harrisonburg, Virginia

EDGEWOOD COLLEGE OF
THE SACRED HEART ††
Madison, Wisconsin

EUREKA COLLEGE
Eureka, Illinois

FINDLAY COLLEGE
Findlay, Ohio

FORT WAYNE BIBLE
COLLEGE
Fort Wayne, Indiana

GEORGE FOX COLLEGE
Newberg, Oregon

GODDARD COLLEGE
Plainfield, Vermont

GORDON COLLEGE
Beverly Farms, Massachusetts

GRAND CANYON COL-
LEGE
Phoenix, Arizona

HILLYER COLLEGE OF THE
UNIVERSITY OF HART-
FORD †
Hartford, Connecticut

HUNTINGTON COLLEGE
Huntington, Indiana

JOHN BROWN UNIVERSITY
Siloam Springs, Arkansas

THE KING'S COLLEGE
Briarcliff Manor, New York

LAKELAND COLLEGE
Sheboygan, Wisconsin

LA MENNAIS COLLEGE
Alfred, Maine

212

LOS ANGELES PACIFIC
COLLEGE
Los Angeles, California

McKENDREE COLLEGE *
Lebanon, Illinois

MADISON COLLEGE
Madison College, Tennessee

MADONNA COLLEGE †
Livonia, Michigan

MALONE COLLEGE *
Canton, Ohio

MARIAN COLLEGE *
Fond du Lac, Wisconsin

MARLBORO COLLEGE
Marlboro, Vermont

MARYMOUNT COLLEGE
Los Angeles, California

MESSIAH COLLEGE
Grantham, Pennsylvania

MILLIGAN COLLEGE
Milligan College, Tennessee

MILTON COLLEGE
Milton, Wisconsin

MONTREAT COLLEGE * ††
Montreat, North Carolina

MORRIS COLLEGE
Sumter, South Carolina

MORRIS HARVEY
COLLEGE ††
Charleston, West Virginia

MOUNT MARTY COL-
LEGE ††
Yankton, South Dakota

NASSON COLLEGE
Springvale, Maine

NATIONAL COLLEGE
Kansas City, Missouri

NEW ENGLAND COLLEGE
Henniker, New Hampshire

NORTHWEST CHRISTIAN
COLLEGE
Eugene, Oregon

OAKLAND CITY COLLEGE
Oakland City, Indiana

OAKWOOD COLLEGE ††
Huntsville, Alabama

OLIVET COLLEGE
Olivet, Michigan

PAUL QUINN COLLEGE
Waco, Texas

PIEDMONT COLLEGE
Demorest, Georgia

PIKEVILLE COLLEGE
Pikeville, Kentucky

PROVIDENCE-BARRINGTON
BIBLE COLLEGE
Providence, Rhode Island

RICKER COLLEGE
Houlton, Maine

RIO GRANDE COLLEGE
Rio Grande, Ohio

ROBERTS WESLEYAN
COLLEGE
North Chili, New York

SACRED HEART COL-
LEGE
Wichita, Kansas

ST. FRANCIS COLLEGE
Biddeford, Maine

ST. FRANCIS COLLEGE †
Brooklyn, New York

ST. JOSEPH ON THE RIO
GRANDE, COLLEGE OF
Albuquerque, New Mexico

ST. JOSEPH'S COLLEGE
North Windham, Maine

ST. MARY, COLLEGE OF ††
Omaha, Nebraska

ST. MARY OF THE PLAINS
COLLEGE
Dodge City, Kansas

ST. MEINRAD SEMINARY
St. Meinrad, Indiana

ST. MICHAEL'S COLLEGE
Santa Fe, New Mexico

SALEM COLLEGE
Salem, West Virginia

SIOUX FALLS COLLEGE ††
Sioux Falls, South Dakota

STEUBENVILLE, COLLEGE
OF
Steubenville, Ohio

TABOR COLLEGE
Hillsboro, Kansas

UPLAND COLLEGE †
Upland, California

WESLEYAN METHODIST
COLLEGE *
Central, South Carolina

WESTERN NEW ENGLAND
COLLEGE
Springfield, Massachusetts

WESTMONT COLLEGE †
Santa Barbara, California

WILBERFORCE UNIVERSITY
Wilberforce, Ohio

WILLIAM JENNINGS BRYAN
COLLEGE
Dayton, Tennessee

WILLIAM PENN COLLEGE
Oskaloosa, Iowa

CASC has experienced a turnover in membership since its founding in April, 1956. The colleges marked * joined CASC in the spring of 1958; those marked † received regional accreditation after joining CASC. At the time this book was printed, the eight colleges marked †† had discontinued their membership. Three new members had been added to the list: Grace College, Winona Lake, Indiana; Mount Mercy College, Cedar Rapids, Iowa; and Nichols College, Dudley, Massachusetts. The statistical material in the text is based on the list of 65 colleges holding membership in the spring of 1959.

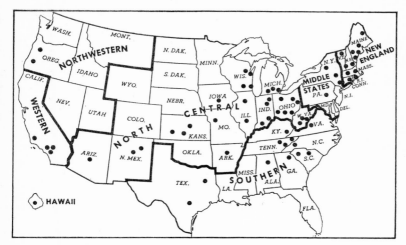

GEOGRAPHICAL DISTRIBUTION OF CASC COLLEGES (SPRING 1959)

CASC has 65 members distributed throughout 31 states. Regional distribution is as follows: Middle States, 4; New England, 12; North Central, 31; Northwestern, 2; Southern, 11; Western, 5. There are 53 coeducational colleges; 7 for women only; 5 for men only. There are 16 Catholic colleges; 9 non-church affiliated; 30 Protestant; and 10 interdenominational.